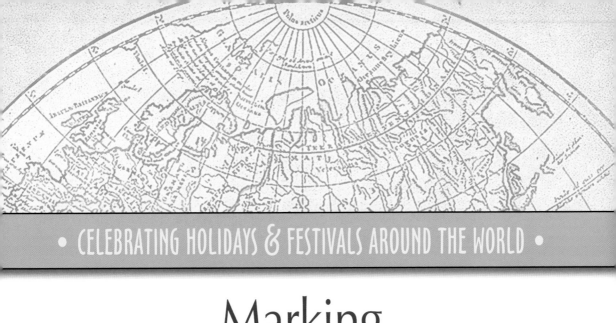

Marking
the Religious New Year

Betsy Richardson

MASON CREST

Mason Crest
450 Parkway Drive, Suite D Broomall, PA 19008
www.masoncrest.com

Printed in the United States of America
First printing
9 8 7 6 5 4 3 2 1

Series ISBN: 978-1-4222-4143-1
Hardcover ISBN: 978-1-4222-4151-6

Library of Congress Cataloging-in-Publication Data is available on file.

Developed and Produced by Print Matters Productions, Inc. (www.printmattersinc.com)
Cover and Interior Design by Lori S Malkin Design LLC

CELEBRATING HOLIDAYS & FESTIVALS AROUND THE WORLD

Carnival

Christmas & Hanukkah

Easter, Passover & Festivals of Hope

Halloween & Remembrances of the Dead

Independence Days

Lent, Yom Kippur & Days of Repentance

Marking the Religious New Year

Ramadan

Ringing in the Western & Chinese New Year

Thanksgiving & Other Festivals of the Harvest

KEY ICONS TO LOOK FOR:

 Words to understand: These words with their easy-to-understand definitions will increase the reader's understanding of the text while building vocabulary skills.

 Sidebars: This boxed material within the main text allows readers to build knowledge, gain insights, explore possibilities, and broaden their perspectives by weaving together additional information to provide realistic and holistic perspectives.

 Educational Videos: Readers can view videos by scanning our QR codes, providing them with additional educational content to supplement the text. Examples include news coverage, moments in history, speeches, iconic sports moments and much more!

 Text-dependent Questions: These questions send the reader back to the text for more careful attention to the evidence presented there.

 Research projects: Readers are pointed toward areas of further inquiry connected to each chapter. Suggestions are provided for projects that encourage deeper research and analysis.

 Series glossary of key terms: This back-of-the book glossary contains terminology used throughout this series. Words found here increase the reader's ability to read and comprehend higher-level books and articles in this field.

CONTENTS

INTRODUCTION

Celebrating Holidays & Festivals Around the World

olidays mark time. They occupy a space outside of ordinary events and give shape and meaning to our everyday existence. They also remind us of the passage of time as we reflect on Christmases, Passovers, or Ramadans past. Throughout human history, nations and peoples have marked their calendars with special days to celebrate, commemorate, and memorialize. We set aside times to reflect on the past and future, to rest and renew physically and spiritually, and to simply have fun.

In English we call these extraordinary moments "holidays," a contraction of the term "holy day." Sometimes holidays are truly holy days–the Sabbath, Easter, or Eid al-Fitr, for example–but they can also be nonreligious occasions that serve political purposes, address the social needs of communities and individuals, or focus on regional customs and games.

This series explores the meanings and celebrations of holidays across religions and cultures around the world. It groups the holidays into volumes according to theme (such as *Lent, Yom Kippur & Days of Repentance*; *Thanksgiving & Other Festivals of the Harvest*; *Independence Days*; *Easter, Passover & Festivals of Hope*; *Ringing in the Western & Chinese New Year*; *Marking the Religious New Year*; *Carnival*; *Ramadan*; and *Halloween & Remembrances of the Dead*) or by their common human experience due to their closeness on the calendar (such as *Christmas & Hanukkah*). Each volume introduces readers to the origins, history, and common practices associated with the holidays before embarking on a worldwide tour that shows the regional variations and distinctive celebrations within specific countries. The reader will learn how these holidays started, what they mean to the people who celebrate them, and how different cultures celebrate them.

◀ A man blows his shofar, a ram's horn, in his backyard in Jackson Hole, Wyoming, as part of his religious observance of the beginning of the Jewish new year, Rosh Hashanah.

These volumes have an international focus, and thus readers will be able to learn about diversity both at home and throughout the world. We can learn a great deal about a people or nation by the holidays they celebrate. We can also learn from holidays how cultures and religions have interacted and mingled over time. We see in celebrations not just the past through tradition, but the principles and traits that people embrace and value today.

The Celebrating Holidays & Festivals Around the World series surveys this rich and varied festive terrain. Its 10 volumes show the distinct ways that people all over the world infuse ordinary life with meaning, purpose, or joy. The series cannot be all-inclusive or the last word on so vast a subject, but it offers a vital first step for those eager to learn more about the diverse, fascinating, and vibrant cultures of the world, through the festivities that give expression, order, and meaning to their lives.

INTRODUCTION

Marking the Religious New Year

New year's celebrations all over the world are times when families and friends come together and celebrate endings and new beginnings. These holidays provide the chance to make a fresh start, welcome a new season, develop a new attitude, or acquire a new outlook on life. When a religious element is added to these celebrations, there is also a sense of spiritual duty. Rather than just "ring in the new year" with food and festivities, religious new year's celebrations invite their participants to slow down and truly consider the meaning of the holiday, the passage of time, and the opportunity for personal change.

Many of the world's religions have new year's celebrations based on their own calendars, each with its own history and set of traditions. For these religions, new year's may occur long after the January 1 date used by the Western world. It comes at a time important to that particular religion for reasons that might stretch back centuries.

While most of the world waits in anticipation on New Year's Eve for the beginning of the upcoming year, religious new year's celebrations are less about the transition from one year to the next than about the spiritual journey from an old self to a new. Particular foods, prayers, and other customs strengthen the sense of this journey. Religious new year's celebrations, such as the Hindu Divali, Jewish Rosh Hashanah, and Muslim Al-Hijra continually return to the theme of personal renewal. They all have a feeling of history and permanence.

Despite the spiritual aspect of religious new year's celebrations, the focus of any new year's celebration–religious and nonreligious alike–remains the passing of time as it relates to the inner realm of a person's attitudes, ideas, and beliefs. Whether a new year's observance is joyous, reflective, boisterous, contemplative, or a combination of all these things, it is an opportunity to examine the past year while preparing for the next, and provides a clear point from which to make a new beginning.

▲ The festival of Divali is fun for children and adults alike. Here, a family celebrates with sparkling fireworks in New Delhi, India.

Origins and Celebrations of Rosh Hashanah

Rosh Hashanah is the Jewish new year celebrated by Jews around the world, especially in Israel and North America, parts of South America, and Europe. It is observed and celebrated on the first day of the Hebrew month Tishri (September or October on the Gregorian calendar). Rosh Hashanah is a time to think back upon the past year and prepare for the upcoming one through reflection, repentance, and prayer. Religious Jews

WORDS TO UNDERSTAND

Gregorian calendar: The solar calendar implemented in 1582 during the papacy of Pope Gregory XIII that includes a leap day every fourth February to keep time with the astronomical seasons.

High Holy Days: The days celebrated by Jewish people everywhere that begin right after the Jewish New Year, Rosh Hashanah, and end 10 days later with Yom Kippur, the Jewish Day of Atonement.

Messiah: A person believed to be the rescuer of a region, a people, or the entire world.

◄ The Hekhal, an ornamental closet that contains each synagogue's Torah scrolls, is often placed on the wall of the temple that faces Jerusalem. The Torah scrolls are removed from the closet and paraded through the congregation for services.

are not supposed to work on Rosh Hashanah and often spend much of the day in their synagogues in services that can be hours long. In Israel, all businesses are closed. Rosh Hashanah is also a time to spend with families and friends, as well as an important time to visit graves of loved ones, as many Jews believe the dead can speak to God for them. Jews have been celebrating Rosh Hashanah for about 2,000 years, or slightly more than half their history.

■ Origins of Rosh Hashanah

Judaism, a religion practiced by people known as Jews, is one of the world's oldest religious traditions. The Jewish people are believed to have descended from the patriarchs (or fathers) Abraham, Isaac, Jacob, and Moses, whose stories are told in the first book of the Torah, or Hebrew Bible. Jews believe in one God who created the universe. Unlike other messianic religions (those that hold out the prospect of a world savior or divine leader), Judaism generally posits that the messiah has yet to appear. In honoring the one god–known variously as Adonai, Yahweh, or the unnameable one–observant Jews keep Sabbath, also called Shabbat, as a day of rest, running from sunset to sunset from Friday to Saturday.

There are currently more than 14 million Jews worldwide. Almost half of the worldwide Jewish community lives in the United States, mostly concentrated on the East Coast and in California. More than 1.5 million Jews live in New York State, which is more than 8 percent of the state's population.

TWO MAJOR GROUPS OF JUDAISM: ORTHODOX AND REFORM JEWS

Variations in Rosh Hashanah celebrations depend on what branch of Judaism is being practiced. The main division in Judaism is between Orthodox Jews, who live their lives by following the Jewish holy books (the Torah, Talmud, and Mishnah) as the unwavering law of God, and Reform Jews, who feel that the holy books provide religious guidance but can also be interpreted as historical documents that must change with the times. Orthodox Jews follow strictly the religious laws as well as the dress and eating codes that are set forth in the Jewish holy books, while Reform Jews dress in modern clothing and are less strict about what they eat.

THE JEWISH CALENDAR

The Jewish calendar, which has been used since 3761 B.C.E., is a lunar calendar with 12 months. Each month has 29 or 30 days, making a year 354 days long. To keep the fall and spring holidays in the correct seasons, an extra month is added every 19 years. For the Jews each day begins at sundown, or dusk, and lasts until the following sundown.

Rosh Hashanah, which literally means "the head of the year," is observed and celebrated on the first of Tishri. In ancient times it was difficult for Jews outside of Jerusalem to be sure of the exact date of the new Moon during Tishri, which begins the holiday, so Rosh Hashanah is usually celebrated for two days both in Israel and in other parts of the world where Jews live. According to the Torah, Tishri, sometimes called Ethanim, is the seventh month in the Jewish calendar. Despite this, the Jewish New Year has been observed and celebrated on the first day of Tishri since ancient times.

■ Celebrating Rosh Hashanah

Jews believe many important events occurred on or after Rosh Hashanah. It is on this day that God created humanity, making it the birthday of the world. It is also the day that Isaac was born to Abraham. Rosh Hashanah marks the time when God revealed to Moses that the first tribes of Jews,

▲ During the Jewish **High Holy Days** (Rosh Hashanah and Yom Kippur), a curtain is hung over the ark that houses the Torahs. Here, Jewish men pray at the ark that houses the Torahs.

or Israelites, would be expelled from their native land of Egypt. In addition, it is considered to be the Day of Judgment, when all people on Earth and those who have already died will be judged by God. The names of the good are written into the Book of Life, the wicked are erased from it, and those in between are given until the holiday of Yom Kippur–10 days after Rosh Hashanah begins–to repent for their sins and be placed alongside the good in the Book of Life. In fact, a common greeting that people say to each other on Rosh Hashanah is *l'shanah tova ti-ka-tey-vu*. This literally means, "May you be inscribed [in the Book of Life] for a good new year." During the month before Tishri called Elul, many Jews spend time in deep reflection and religious study. This is part of their preparation for Rosh Hashanah. The terms of the holiday are laid out in the third book of the Hebrew scriptures, Leviticus. (The Hebrew scriptures are called Tanakh; they contain the same body of works as the Old Testament in the Christian Bible. The first five books of the Tanakh make up the Torah, known also as the Books of Moses and as the Pentateuch.) For Rosh Hashanah it is specified, "In the seventh month, in the first day of the month, there shall be a solemn rest for you, a sacred convocation commemorated with the blast of the ram's horn. You shall not work at any of your ordinary labor, and you shall bring a fire offering to the Lord." (Lev. 23:23–25)

BLESSING THE CANDLES

A Shehechiyanu blessing is recited before lighting the Rosh Hashanah candles just before sundown at the end of the first day of the celebration. The Hebrew words for the blessing are: *Baruch atah Ado-nai, Ehlohaynu melech Ha-olam, she'he'che'yanu v'kee'manu, v'hee'gee'anu la'zman ha'zeh*. "Blessed are you Lord, our God, ruler of the world, who has kept us alive, sustained us, and enabled us to reach this season."

CANDLES AND WORSHIP

Preliminary rituals for Rosh Hashanah take place in the homes of Jewish families at sunset on the evening before the new year. It starts with the lighting of candles that signify the beginning of the festival, and then by saying a blessing before going off to a place of worship. If the Jewish community is large, as it is in Israel and many parts of the United States, Rosh Hashanah is celebrated in the place of Jewish worship called a synagogue. If it is a small Jewish community, the Rosh Hashanah service might take place in the basement of a Christian church, a community center, or even someone's living room. Jews attend rounds of services over the holiday, from the first to the last evening services and morning and afternoon services in between.

THE SHOFAR

Rosh Hashanah begins with the blowing of a shofar, or ram's horn, to signal the start of holiday observances. An evening service is held during which the rabbi or other church leader reads from the prayer book called the *Machzor*, used exclusively on the Jewish High Holy Days. The evening service is not usually long. Afterward, families go home to eat together and sometimes invite others to eat with them.

SWEET AND ROUND FOODS

For Rosh Hashanah, foods have special significance. Many of the foods should be sweet for a sweet year, round to symbolize the year's cycle, and abundant for prosperity and productivity. Families traditionally prepare for the day by making and praying over loaves of sweet, soft challah–round braided bread made with eggs to symbolize the cycle of life. At holiday meals they eat the challah with apples dipped in honey, signaling their hope for a sweet new year.

THE ANCIENT CALL

The shofar has a long history in Judaism that began thousands of years ago and continues today. It was used to signal Shabbat. It was also used to declare the crowning of a new king. Today the shofar is still sounded at the swearing in of a new Israeli president, and on Rosh Hashanah it signifies a call to repentance and awakening. Each day of Rosh Hashanah, the shofar is blown 100 times. However, if a holiday falls on Shabbat it is not blown.

Listen to a shofar being blown on Rosh Hashanah.

As part of the Rosh Hashanah feast, Jewish families will prepare and serve a stew or casserole called tzimmes made of carrots, cinnamon, yams, prunes, and honey. The carrots are an important ingredient of the recipe, since the word for carrots in Yiddish (a Judeo-German language), *merren*, also means "more." Everyone yearns for more of something on the Jewish new year: more wealth, more knowledge, more good deeds, and even more children. The carrots in this tasty dish are sliced into small round coin-like shapes, and eating them is thought to be a good forecast for prosperity. Another popular food tradition is to eat a fish or sheep's head. The head stands for the desire to be at the head of whatever one does, as opposed to the tail.

A selection of symbolic foods that have a place in the classic Rosh Hashanah meal includes a round loaf of challah bread (top left) topped with apples dipped in honey. Around the challah are honey, pomegranates, and an apple.

Sour or bitter foods are avoided during Rosh Hashanah, and most observant Jews (those who actively practice the religion of Judaism) also avoid nuts because the word in Hebrew for nut—*egoz*—has the same numeric value as the word *chet*, which means "sin" in Hebrew.

After the final services of Rosh Hashanah there is a large feast to formally welcome the new year. A special blessing is recited called Shehechiyanu that thanks God for giving sustenance to his people. After the blessing Jews eat a fruit that has not yet been eaten that season.

CASTING SINS INTO THE SEA

An ancient ritual of Rosh Hashanah that has survived to modern times is called *tashlik*, which means, "You will cast." In this ritual a congregation or small group gathers after the last of the formal holiday services at a body of water that varies depending on the area of the country or world in which one lives—it could be an ocean, a river, or a small stream. A rabbi or other congregation leader reads the Torah verse, "And you will cast all their sins into the depths of the sea." Those in the congregation empty their pockets of breadcrumbs or throw small stones into the water to symbolically cleanse themselves of their sins. In some areas, Jews may plunge together into the waters to perform the ritual. Other readings during the ritual include prayers

▲ Jews gather at a lake in Minnesota to cast bread upon the water, an ancient custom representing the casting off of sins.

from the Book of Micha. Micha was a Jewish prophet who wrote about *teshuva*, which means repentance.

ORTHODOX ROSH HASHANAH

During Rosh Hashanah, the differences between Reform Jews and Orthodox Jews become apparent in their holiday rituals and services. For example, in many Jewish places of worship singers are often accompanied by organs and other instruments on Rosh Hashanah and other holidays. However, Orthodox Jews do not permit the use of musical instruments on the Shabbat or during festivals, including Rosh Hashanah. Orthodox men and women worship separately in the synagogue, and women are often seated in the balcony. On the day before Rosh Hashanah, Orthodox men and women take ritual baths called *mikvah*. This is thought to purify the spirit for the period of atonement that begins with Rosh Hashanah.

▲ This honey cake has double symbolism. It is sweet with honey for a sweet new year and round to symbolize the circle of life.

TEXT-DEPENDENT QUESTIONS

1: What is the name of the Jewish new year?

2: Name one of the Jewish patriarchs.

3: What happens during the ritual of *tashlik*?

RESEARCH PROJECTS

1: Research the Jewish holy books, the Torah, Talmud, and Mishnah. Write a brief synopsis of what each book includes, its function and role in the Jewish tradition, and other noteworthy facts about its composition and history.

2: Research the Karaite sect of Judaism, including its history, beliefs and customs, noteworthy figures, and contemporary traditions. Write a brief report summarizing your findings, including information on where their modern communities are based.

◄ Jews pray at the Western Wall in Jerusalem's Old City during the two-day festival of Rosh Hashanah that marks the beginning of the Jewish new year.

Origins and Celebrations of Divali

Divali is the Hindu festival of lights. For many Hindus it also marks the beginning of a new year. It is celebrated by Hindus in India and throughout the **diaspora**, or the many other parts of the world where Hindu Indians live. Divali is the most important holiday of the year for Hindus everywhere. It is also celebrated by Jains and by Sikhs, two religious groups with roots in Hinduism. For most Hindus, Divali celebrates the victory of good over evil in the world. It involves numerous rituals and festivities that honor family and friends, as well as the many deities (gods) that make up the Hindu pantheon (the Hindu group of gods). No one is certain when Divali first took place. Many believe the earliest celebrations began almost 3,500 years ago.

WORDS TO UNDERSTAND

Diaspora: The scattering of a culture or group of people who share ethnic origins when they settle outside of their native country.
Karma: A Hindu belief that the value of somebody's life now and in the future is directly related to that person's behavior and conduct in past lives.
Personification: Giving a nonhuman thing human traits or actions.

◀ Divali, the Hindu festival of lights, is the most important Hindu holiday.

ONE RIVER, TWO STREAMS

The blending of religious practices and beliefs from more than one culture is called *syncretism*. Syncretism occurs when two or more societies live and work together in the same area. Over time, with intermarriage and sociopolitical interaction (when groups work out how to share society), new belief systems emerge that have characteristics of both religions.

■ Origins of Divali

THE HINDU RELIGION

Hinduism is the religion of the majority of Indians. It was created more than 4,000 years ago as a mixture of different religious traditions present in India. Nomadic tribes–or people who move together in groups from place to place and bring with them different customs, traditions, and beliefs–also influenced its development. Today it is practiced by an estimated 950 million people around the world.

The Hindu pantheon is vast. In fact, there are 330 million deities that a Hindu can worship. Above all of these is a Supreme Being Hindus refer to as the one God, or Brahman. The Supreme Being is the universal creative force that guides all living things on Earth. Each Hindu god or goddess represents a particular characteristic of the Supreme Being. They are **personifications**, or earthly representations, of Brahman. Just as people usually have several different roles in life, such as son, daughter, student, or friend, Brahman is called different things depending on which role he is fulfilling or performing. Of the many gods and goddesses under Brahman, the three most important ones are Brahma, Vishnu, and Shiva. Each one represents one of Brahman's main roles: Brahma is the creator of the universe, Vishnu is the preserver and protector of the universe, and Shiva is the destroyer.

Hindus direct prayers to specific gods and goddesses depending on their needs and the role of that god or goddess. For example, Sarasvati is the goddess of wisdom and learning. She is the representation of all knowledge–art, science, crafts, and skills. She is not often worshipped in the temples, but she is a favorite of school students, artists, and people who work with their hands. In addition, there are thousands of local gods who watch over cities, towns, and families. People from different regions pray to different local gods to give them things like good weather and healthy crops.

THE HINDU CALENDAR

The main difference between the Hindu calendar and the Gregorian calendar (the calendar most widely used around the world today) is that the Hindu calendar is a lunar calendar, one that follows

▲ A group of Malaysian Hindu men and women recite prayers during Divali celebrations at a Hindu temple in Delhi, India. Divali is the most important festival of the year for Hindus around the world.

the cycles of the Moon, and the Gregorian calendar is a solar calendar, one that follows the cycles of the Sun. The Gregorian calendar measures the year as 365 1/4 days, or one rotation of Earth around the Sun. The Hindu calendar measures the year in 12 rotations of the Moon around Earth, called lunar cycles. The first day of the new year, or Divali, is celebrated on a different day every year. For most Hindus who live in or are originally from India, Divali takes place on the first new Moon in the Hindu month of Kartikka. (This Hindu month corresponds to the months of October and November on the Gregorian calendar.)

■ Celebrating Divali

Of the hundreds of holidays celebrated by Hindus each year, Divali is the most significant. Given the complexity of the Hindu religion and culture, especially the number of gods and goddesses whose worship is emphasized in a particular region or country, it is not surprising that over the centuries Divali has expanded beyond one day. In fact, Divali is usually a five-day experience with corresponding rituals and customs for each day.

Divali is celebrated as both a religious and a national holiday in India. During Divali, families everywhere will honor the Hindu gods and goddesses by exchanging gifts, eating elaborate meals, and enjoying fireworks displays. Indian business leaders who hope for a prosperous year will also open new account books at this time.

PREPARING FOR DIVALI

A major part of Divali preparations and subsequent celebration is the thorough cleaning of the home, crowned by the creation of elaborate designs called *rangoli* on

Watch the creation of a *rangoli* design.

the floors and walls. Hindu women use rice powder, crushed white stone, or colored chalk to make these designs, then add grain, beads, flowers, or other found materials for further decoration. In southern India, it is common to use flowers and leaves from marigolds and chrysanthemums to make the *rangoli* look three-dimensional.

To make a *rangoli*, one begins by sprinkling the powder by hand, allowing just a little to fall at a time. This makes an outline of dots that are then joined with other materials to form a pattern. It is important that the entire pattern be made of unbroken lines so no evil spirits can enter through the gaps. Many *rangoli* patterns are handed down through generations and some are hundreds of years old. Circular designs are popular because they symbolize the endlessness of time. Other *rangoli* themes include the Sun, Moon, and stars. In some Indian regions the images of fish, birds, elephants, flowers, and vines are more prominent.

One major *rangoli* theme is the lotus flower, a Hindu symbol of beauty, prosperity, and fertility. In addition, the goddess Lakshmi is often shown holding or sitting on a lotus blossom. Since she is the most important deity of the Divali celebration, her image is often incorporated into *rangoli* design. She is usually depicted as dramatic and colorful, draped in red-and-gold clothes. She is represented with four arms and four hands. Each of these hands represents a different Hindu virtue: *dharma*, or righteousness; *kama*, which means genuine desire; *artha*, or wealth; and *moksha*, freedom from the cycle of birth and death that keeps a person attached to the world and prevents him or her from the ultimate goal of becoming divine. Usually one element of the *rangoli* is a series of small footsteps leading to the entrance of a home or business. The footprints represent a path that welcomes Lakshmi and shows her the way.

▲ Vendors sell small packets of colored powder used for decorating homes during the Hindu festival of Divali in Ahmadabad, India.

■ The Five Days of Divali

Each day of Divali highlights a different aspect of the celebration. The first day is known as Dhanteras. This is when Hindus typically buy new clothes and get rid of old, worn ones. It is also customary to buy something made of gold or silver, since metallic objects are supposed to bring good luck. On the night of Dhanteras, Hindu families light the first *diyas,* or devotional candles, in their homes and pray together to summon the gods they hope will descend upon them. This is a necessary moment of repose before what will be a flurry of activity in the days ahead. It centers the family and reminds them of the true intention of the holiday.

THE SECOND DAY OF DIVALI

At sunrise on the second day of Divali, many Hindus bathe themselves in oils as part of a ritual cleansing to wash away the evils of their sins, just as days before they washed the interiors of their homes. This ritual bathing is especially common in northern India. On this day Hindus will also offer food to whichever goddess is associated with their place of origin, and sometimes to their ancestors to help bring them good luck. The second day of Divali is often referred to as Choti Divali or "little Divali," since it comes just before the main Divali celebration.

Hindus believe that on the second evening of Divali, known also as Kali Chaudas or Bhoot Chatur, Shiva the Destroyer arrives accompanied by his band of ghouls and wicked spirits who delight in causing chaos and destruction. Hindus use this second evening to meditate on their belief that Shiva embodies the good and bad in all of humanity. He is perceived as gentle and fierce, creative as well as destructive. Hindus consider him an important and necessary part of an imperfect world. The remainder of the second day of Divali is used to prepare for the third and most important day.

THE THIRD DAY OF DIVALI

The third day of Divali is the day Hindus welcome the goddess Lakshmi into their homes to bring blessings and good fortune. They do this by spending hours making a variety of rich foods and sweets such as *kheer*–a creamy pudding made with rice, rice flakes, or sago (sago is a powdery starch made from sago palms). Spicy lentil fritters typically accompany the *kheer*. Other dishes, such as chicken masala, are also popular. While dishes for Divali share common spices, such as ginger, coriander, and turmeric, every Hindu community has its unique variation on each of the recipes.

Perhaps the most beautiful ritual of Divali is the lighting of thousands of lights, called *diyas*, inside homes all over towns and cities with Hindu communities. Coming into their full glory on the third night of Divali, these lights represent the symbolic inner light that comes from spiritual purification as well as the illuminating force of good over evil. They also brighten the path for important Hindu deities who are returning to be welcomed in Hindu homes. For many Hindus, the most important of these deities is Lakshmi. She is believed to be the wife of Vishnu, the preserver and protector of the universe, and is the goddess of wealth, love, beauty, and good fortune. One day of the Divali celebration is entirely devoted to praying to her to ensure a year of happiness and prosperity.

Finally, Hindus everywhere are ready to welcome the goddess. When the sky is at its darkest and the new Moon is cresting in the sky, families light their *diyas* so Lakshmi can find her way to their homes. Some families also leave their windows open so that she will be sure to find a way to enter. To open one's home to her, or to any of the millions of gods and ancestral spirits called upon during Divali, is to signify a person's openness to the future and trust in both the goodness of the self and the goodness of the outside world.

▲ A woman lights oil lamps for Divali celebrations in Ahmadabad, India. The lights represent the inner light of spiritual purification and the force of good over evil, while also brightening the path for Hindu deities as they make their way into Hindu homes.

Indoors families decorate altars for Lakshmi. They offer her a silver platter filled with fruit, flowers, puffed rice, and silver coins. One *diya* has the place of honor in the center. Since Hindus believe that Lakshmi was born in a turbulent ocean of milk, and holding a lotus flower, Lakshmi coins and figures are lovingly bathed in milk and then decorated with vermilion, a bright red dye similar to the color of lotus flowers. On this night, the father of the home frequently reads from the sacred Ramayana texts, and the mother leads prayers and songs for success and prosperity. After a period of devotional time around the altar, Hindus gather outside in their villages, towns, and cities for feasting, music.

THE FOURTH DAY OF DIVALI

The fourth day of Divali is the official new year. The particular legend of the Hindu god Krishna that is celebrated on the fourth day of Divali relates to the rural area in which he is said to have lived near Mount Govardhana in the north Indian state of Uttar Pradesh. The local farmers there are said to have offered thanks to Indra, the God of rain and storms, every year. For their annual pilgrimage, they traveled to the mountain to make offerings to Indra for help in making their crops grow. But Indra had not helped them for several years, and the farmers' crops suffered. One particular year,

▲ Children light sparklers to celebrate the Divali festival in New Delhi, India.

the local cow herder's child, Krishna, went with the farmers as they headed toward the mountain. Krishna did not agree with giving offerings to Indra. He asked why Indra deserved their thanks if he had brought no rain. Krishna said that it made more sense to offer prayers and food–a ritual called *puja*–to the fields, the mountain, and the sacred cows. After all, the mountain protected them, the cows helped the farmers with their planting, and the fields provided them soil for crops.

The farmers were soon persuaded by the young Krishna and began *puja*, preparations for the cows and mountain. Seeing this, Indra became enraged at what he took to be a great insult. To punish the

THE LAW OF KARMA

Reincarnation is the Hindu belief that when a human or an animal dies, its soul is reborn in a different body (other thought systems also include a belief in reincarnation). A soul can be reborn many times in many different bodies. How well or badly someone lives their life will determine what kind of animal or person they will be in the next life. This accumulated good or bad behavior is known as *karma*.

people and demonstrate his power, he unleashed a terrible storm of heavy rain and lightning. It rained for days. The downpour threatened not only to wash away the people and the cows but also to flood the fields on which their crops depended. The frightened people ran to Krishna for help. The amazing young Krishna, using only his little finger, lifted Mount Govardhana and held it in the air, allowing the farmers and cattle to take shelter underneath. Krishna held up the mountain for seven full days, until a humbled Indra was forced to relent, stop the rain, and pay his respects to Krishna. Indra understood then that Krishna was indeed a true god worthy of respect.

THE FIFTH DAY OF DIVALI

The final day of Divali is known as Bhai Dooj, or Brother's Day. On this day sisters and brothers lavish attention on one another. If a family does not have a daughter, the son might spend time with a female cousin or with a friend. Brothers go to the home of their sisters to eat a meal prepared just for them. The sister paints the traditional *tilak*, a sacred red mark Hindus wear, on her brother's forehead to show her love and give him her protection. Sisters might also pray for their brothers' prosperity and health, and toss rice on them for good luck. The brothers will give their sisters presents–sometimes presented on a silver platter–of jewelry, sweets, or even clothes. Schools remain closed on this final day of Divali. This is true throughout India as well as in other places with large Hindu populations such as Malaysia, Sri Lanka, and Nepal. On this final night of the holiday, families may gather for enormous fireworks displays that last well into the night.

READING THE RAMAYANA EPIC

Hindus everywhere learn about the deeds of their central gods by reading the four sacred Hindu texts, called Vedas. The Vedas are collections of the stories, teachings, rules, and beliefs of Hinduism. During Divali, parents and grandparents might read an epic tale from the Vedas, called the Ramayana, to their children. Like the Christian Bible or the Muslim Quran, the Ramayana and other sacred Hindu texts provide lessons on good behavior for mothers, fathers, sisters, and brothers, as well as how to treat people outside the family. It is thus a fitting text to read at the beginning of the new year, when families are open to thinking about and improving the moral character of their lives.

In the Ramayana tale, the god Vishnu is reincarnated (reborn into a different body) into the form of Rama. It is believed that Rama is the seventh reincarnation of Vishnu's soul. Rama makes a long journey during which he kills demons, helps the poor, listens to the advice of sages, and accomplishes many other heroic deeds. At the end of his journey he frees his wife Sita from the demon king Ravana. When he returns to his home city of Ayodhya he is crowned king for ridding the world of evil.

 TEXT-DEPENDENT QUESTIONS

1: What two other religious groups besides Hindus celebrate Divali?

2: What day of Divali is the official new year?

3: What is the name of the four sacred Hindu texts?

RESEARCH PROJECTS

1: Research the *Mahabharata*, an epic poem of the Hindu tradition. Write a brief summary of its history, major plot points, and relationship to the Hindu faith. If possible, include how it is similar or different to the Ramayana, another Hindu epic.

2: Research another Hindu holiday. Examples include Holi, Navratri, or Maha Shivaratri. Write a brief description of this holiday, including information about its date, significance to Hindu religion and culture, and ways that Hindus observe it.

▲ A wall painting shows a scene from the Ramayana epic in Bangkok, Thailand.

Origins and Celebrations of Al-Hijra

Al-Hijra is the new year's holiday celebrated by Muslims around the world. Muslims are followers of the religion of Islam, which means "submission to the will of God." The festival, which is also known as El am Hejir, Ras al Sana, and Muharram, takes place during the Islamic month of Muharram, which corresponds to January and February on the Gregorian calendar. Al-Hijra marks the time that the prophet Muhammad was

WORDS TO UNDERSTAND

Caliph: A Muslim ruler whose claim to leadership is based on being a successor to Muhammad.

Exile: To be forced to move from one's original home or residence as a form of punishment or a personal choice made for political or religious reasons.

Fast: To choose not to eat food, or certain foods, for a period of days, or during parts of a day, often for religious reasons.

Pagan: A person or group who does not believe in one god, but many gods who are closely connected to nature and the natural world.

◀ A Muslim family walks among the crowds in London's Trafalgar Square. More than 1.5 million Muslims live in the United Kingdom.

forced to flee from Mecca to the town of Yathrib (later renamed Medina, which means "City of the Prophet"), where he formed the first Islamic state. Although it is not as significant in the Islamic calendar as Rosh Hashanah or Divali are in the Jewish and Hindu calendars, Al-Hijra is still an important time of historical reflection for the 1 billion Sunni Muslims who live worldwide.

Origins of Al-Hijra

Islam is a religion based on the teachings of the prophet Muhammad. Muhammad was born in the city of Mecca, in what is now Saudi Arabia. At the age of 40 Muhammad had a vision of the archangel Gabriel who revealed to him the divine word of God. His written record of this revelation would become the Quran, the holy text of Islam.

▲ **Egyptian Muslims celebrate the Islamic New Year in front of al-Hussein mosque in Cairo. Al-Hijra is only observed as the Islamic New Year by Sunni Muslims.**

After this revelation Muhammad began preaching around Mecca to all who would listen. His message was that people needed to repent for their sins through prayer, charity, and a belief in one God called Allah. Among Muhammad's audience were members of the powerful tribe to which he belonged, the Quraysh. The Quraysh were influential merchants who controlled a holy site in Mecca called the Kaaba. The Quraysh worshipped many gods represented by sacred stones they placed inside the Kaaba. Muhammad disagreed with this for two reasons. First, he believed that there was only one god. Second, he felt the Quraysh were performing idolatry, or the worship of symbols of God instead of God himself.

MUHAMMAD'S EXILE AND VICTORY

Muhammad was forced to flee from Mecca to the town of Yathrib. While there he acquired more new followers and strengthened his influence over them. Muhammad continued to struggle for power with the pagans of Mecca he had left behind. Eventually, after winning enough support from his new region and forming the original nation of Islam, he was able to take control over Mecca and the ancient Kaaba shrine. He quickly destroyed all the false idols, sacred stones, and religious symbols he had preached against from the start. Muhammad claimed Mecca by using his considerable negotiating skills rather than going to war, preventing a great deal of bloodshed on both sides. Soon his influence began to spread beyond Mecca and Medina. A century after his death in 632 C.E., Islam had spread to all the Middle Eastern countries as well as parts of India, Africa, and Spain.

SHII AND SUNNI MUSLIMS

After Muhammad's death, practicing Muslims divided into two groups over the question of who should lead the Muslim people. The first group, the Shiis, believed Muhammad's only rightful successor (or caliph) was his direct descendant. The second, called the Sunnis, believed that this ruler should be chosen from the community at large. This division of Muslims was made permanent in 680 after a famous battle known as the Battle of Karbala occurred between the Shii and the Sunni

ONE WORD, MANY PEOPLE

Allah is the word for "God" in Arabic. It is used to refer to God, not only by Muslims but also by Christians and Jews who live in countries where Arabic is spoken. The Spanish expression *¡Ojalá!*, which can be loosely translated as "if Allah wills it so," clearly shows the influence of the 800 years that Arabs occupied Spain. Today *¡Ojalá!* expresses a strong desire.

▲ **Muslim women buy cookies as a treat for their families for Al-Hijra at a market in Kuala Lumpur, Malaysia.**

groups. During the battle, the grandson of Muhammad, Imam Hussein, and his troops were defeated by troops sent by the Sunni caliph Yazid I. The bodies of Hussein and his followers were mutilated and Hussein himself beheaded, marking the beginning of the tensions between the Sunnis and the Shiis in the Middle East and in Asia, the effects of which can still be felt today. For Shiis, Al-Hijra is the start of the mourning period for 10 or more days in remembrance of Hussein.

In many regions and for many centuries, Sunni and Shii Muslims often lived and worked together harmoniously or with little conflict. In recent years, however, the old tensions between these two groups have resurfaced and led to the violent division of towns and regions along religious and ethnic lines. This is particularly true in countries such as Iraq, where major political upheavals have occurred.

THE ISLAMIC CALENDAR

The year of Muhammad's forced **exile** was 622 C.E. To commemorate the suffering of Muhammad and his first followers, this became the first year of the Islamic calendar. The Islamic calendar is a lunar calendar that is also called the Hijra calendar. It has 12 months of 29 days each, which means that it is consistently shorter than the Gregorian calendar. Because the Islamic calendar is based on the Quran, it is sacred for Muslims who must observe it properly. For many Muslim countries, the Hijra calendar is the official calendar. In others, the Gregorian calendar is used for civil events and the Hijra calendar is used for religious ones. The month of Muharram, which literally means "mourning," is when the Islamic calendar begins.

Learn more about the Islamic calendar.

A HOLY DESTINATION

The Kaaba at Mecca is the most important pilgrimage site for Muslims. Making the pilgrimage at least one time is one of the Five Pillars of Islam that all Muslims must accomplish before they die. It is expected that all Muslims make the journey if they are financially and physically capable. The Kaaba itself is a one-room structure at the center of the Sacred Mosque. Its four corners roughly face the directions of the compass. The mosque, known as al Masjid al-Haram, is the largest in the world at approximately 60 feet high and 60 feet in length. Five times a day a billion or more Muslims around the world face the direction of Mecca and the Kaaba and pray to Allah.

Celebrating Al-Hijra

Al-Hijra is, by comparison to other secular and sacred new year's festivals, a relatively quiet celebration. Muslims spend much of the month of Muharram in quiet prayer and study. They may reflect upon the history of their religion, the forced emigration of Muhammad and his followers in particular. Often Muslims will gather in mosques (sacred places of worship for a Muslim community) to read portions of the Quran and discuss specific changes in their lives they would like to make. The story of Muhammad's flight from Mecca to Medina is retold orally, sometimes multiple times by different members of the religious community. A fairly recent custom is for families to send cards to one another, a practice many see as influenced by holiday celebrations of the West.

ASHURA: A DAY OF MOURNING

While it is not, strictly speaking, a new year's observance, the 10th day is the defining day of the month of Muharram for close to 15 percent of all Muslims worldwide. Traditionally the 10th day of Muharram, known as Ashura, was declared by Muhammad to be a day of fasting in remembrance

◀ Shii Muslims in Istanbul, Turkey attend an Ashura mourning ceremony to commemorate the martyrdom of Imam Hussein, the grandson of the Prophet Muhammad.

of Noah leaving the ark and Moses being saved from the Egyptians by Allah. While it is no longer a mandatory day of fasting, many Sunni Muslims voluntarily do so to commemorate these two important events. They are important not only for the history of Islam, but Christianity and Judaism as well.

For Shii Muslims Ashura holds an even more profound significance. On this date Shii Muslims gather to lament the death of Imam Hussein with elaborate processions and other mourning rituals. While the Sunnis do not believe in outward displays of emotion, the Shiis do, and their Ashura observances are steeped in noticeable displays of grief.

TEXT-DEPENDENT QUESTIONS

1: During what Islamic month does Al-Hijra take place?

2: According to Islamic tradition, how old was Muhammad when he had a vision of the archangel Gabriel?

3: How many days are in each month of the Islamic calendar?

RESEARCH PROJECTS

1: Research the Five Pillars of Islam. Create a chart or outline of the Five Pillars, including their Arabic and English names, how the faithful observe them, and other notable details.

2: Research an historical figure of Islam. It may be a spiritual figure such as Abu Bakr, a literary figure or poet such as Rumi, or a modern-day figure such as Malcolm X. Write a brief biography of this person, highlighting his or her origins, contributions to the Islam and the world at large, and other details.

Origins and Celebrations of Matariki

The new year traditions of Rosh Hashanah, Divali, and Al-Hijra are part of religious traditions practiced by billions all over Earth. Their exact dates are tied to the lore, holy books, and historical and mythical legends created and perpetuated by the followers of these religions. Around the world some **indigenous** groups, or traditional clans and tribes with ancient ties to the land, celebrate the beginning of the new year in ways quite distinct from the larger communities in which they live.

WORDS TO UNDERSTAND

Genealogy: The study of family lineages and histories.
Indigenous: Something that, or someone who, originates in a region or country or has an ancient relationship to it.
Rite: A traditional and often serious ceremony or custom performed by a community, often a religious group.

◀ A Maori warrior from the local tribe Tu Wharetoa performs a war song on the shore of Lake Taupo in New Zealand for guests.

however, that changed. Almost all the games and traditions of the Maori disappeared. Even some Europeans felt that the missionaries had gone too far, accusing them of "repressing harmless recreations among the natives." In 1839, an American voyager named Wilkes wrote that, "Social amusements are prohibited by severe penalties, though the people are evidently fond of them." (Wilkes 1845) By 1940, Matariki celebrations had largely disappeared, taking with them the yearly festival during which kite making was at its most inventive.

Today the Maori are rediscovering and reviving the role of kites and their incredible kite-making abilities that have a direct and deeply spiritual link to their Matariki celebrations. This is often encouraged by and helped along with the expressed aid of outside organizations eager to learn and spread rich cultural information to the larger community. Sometimes, the eagerness is also for the tourist dollars a region or a country hopes to attract.

REFLECTION

Many Maori elders, not unlike those from Jewish, Hindu, and Muslim communities the world over, are using the days before, during, and after the new year as a crucial period of reflection. It is a time to impart their history and to instruct the next generations in the traditions that connect the past to the future. As important as this is for all religious groups, for particular groups it is sometimes critical to the survival of their indigenous identity.

 TEXT-DEPENDENT QUESTIONS

1: From what country do the Maori hail?

2: How do the Maori determine when their religious new year, Matariki, takes place?

3: What do ethnographers study?

1: Thinking about the Maori's use of genealogy to shape their worldview, research what you can of your own family history. You may choose to interview a parent or grandparent to gain initial information about your family's origins, when they arrived to your current country, and what fields of work they were active in. Write a brief summary of what you've discovered, including important names and dates. Bonus: Create a family tree that visually represents your genealogy.

2: Research the art of the Maori, including weaving, carving, and contemporary painting. Write a brief synopsis of these different forms of expression and how the Maori have used them throughout the centuries.

◀ Maori warriors perform a ceremonial dance in Waitangi, New Zealand.

5

Celebrating in Asia

The continent with the greatest diversity of religious new year's celebrations is Asia. With one-third of the Earth's land and three-fifths of its people, Asia is the largest continent in the world. It is also the most complex. Made up of a multitude of cultures and religions, including Hinduism, Islam, Buddhism, Christianity, and Judaism, it is a place where various traditions must live side-by-side, each working to preserve its own individuality while respecting that of the others around it.

Most of the world is familiar with the Chinese New Year, a 15-day festival featuring parades, fireworks, and a multitude of outdoor festivities. However, Asia is also home to

WORDS TO UNDERSTAND

Buddhism: A world religion and a way of living that is based on the life and teachings of Gautama Buddha, a spiritual leader from ancient India who probably lived around the time of Christ's birth.

Nirvana: For Buddhists and Hindus, the level of enlightenment when a person is no longer reincarnated and thus freed from the endless cycle of birth and rebirth as well as all connection to the material world.

Reverence: To show and feel a deep respect and admiration for someone or some thing.

◀ Hindus decorate stands to hold the oil lamps, known as *diyas*, for the Divali festival of lights.

many other religious new year observances that occur at roughly the same time as the Chinese New Year and have elements in common with Divali. In Vietnam and South Korea, for example, Tet Nguyen and Seollal are elaborate celebrations that honor both living family members and the ancestral spirits and ancient gods that watch over these families during the year. Amid the variety of celebrations, Divali is the most commonly and colorfully celebrated.

The variations in Divali festivals practiced by Hindus, Sikhs, and Jains are pronounced in several Asian countries. The most notable of these are India, Nepal, Malaysia, Sri Lanka, Singapore, Indonesia, and Thailand. Most Divali celebrations in these countries are similar, only with a focus on gods more specific to the nation, region, or community.

Although Islam is usually associated with the Middle Eastern countries where Muhammad founded it, Muslims make up a significant part of the population of several Asian countries as well. Originally coming to different parts of Asia as traders as well as conquerors, they remain in large numbers in several South Asian countries such as India, Pakistan, Indonesia, and Malaysia. While a substantial majority of Indians in India are Hindu and celebrate Divali, more than 170 million Indian citizens practice Islam and celebrate an entirely different new year, Al-Hijra, a full two to three months after the last day of Divali.

For most Asian Muslims, the celebration of Al-Hijra is a day to relate the story of Muhammad's flight, make new year's resolutions, and go to the mosque to pray. Devout Muslims will often give money to the poor on this day, as well as provide food for those who need it. It is a much less elaborate celebration than the Hindu Divali and mostly used as a time to reflect and remember Muhammad's exile from Mecca.

◼ Divali in India

The significance of Divali for the Hindus of India is as diverse as the region itself. India alone has 15 recognized languages, and Hindu India has more than 300 million deities worshipped by close to a billion Hindus. In such a sprawling, complicated environment, Divali celebrations vary from region to region so that each small community can preserve a piece of its original heritage. While there are some common oral traditions for a majority of Hindus recounted during this time, in some areas of India the central focus of Divali is on a local god or goddess who

Experience scenes of Divali in India.

Steamed rice cakes wrapped in coconut leaves and served with chicken or meat curry are an Indonesian Al-Hijra delicacy.

is meaningful to that particular village. For villagers in the south, Divali is also a time to bless and honor the sacred cows. Cows are not only the source of the farmer's livelihood but are also believed to be incarnations of different gods, including both Vishnu and Lakshmi. In India it is forbidden to eat cows. Hindus believe that feeding a cow brings good luck, and killing a cow is an offense punishable by time in jail. During Divali Indians offer traditional Divali sweets to their cows.

PREPARING FOR DIVALI

There is a festive and busy atmosphere as the people prepare for Divali in Mumbai, the largest city in India. All over the city, Hindu families whitewash and paint their homes

ANOTHER FESTIVAL OF LIGHTS

Buddhists of Myanmar (formerly Burma) celebrate a festival of lights similar to Divali. Their three-day holiday commemorates the return of the Buddha from a celestial trip during which he gave lessons to celestial beings before bringing them back with him. As with Divali celebrations in India, Buddhists mark the return of their prophet by lighting their homes, holding festivities in the streets, and paying respects to their elders and the Buddha.

and businesses. Inside the houses, parents and children alike are scrubbing every inch of their bedrooms, living rooms, and kitchens. This is not a normal housecleaning, but an important ritual that helps Hindus prepare for the arrival of Lakshmi, the goddess of prosperity. Legend says that she will come to the cleanest and most inviting Indian homes to bestow good fortune for the coming year. These month-long preparations help families anticipate the jubilant and sacred celebration of Divali. Celebrants hope that by making the outward, physical space clean and new, one also refreshes the internal space of hopes and aspirations.

This scene in Mumbai, a city with more than 18 million people, is repeated throughout the homes of India's more-than 1 billion residents. In addition to their thorough housecleaning, Indian Hindus prepare for Divali by clearing away unwanted garments, household items, or toys, in order to prepare for the possibilities the new year may bring. This is also when the thousands of small oil lamps made of clay called *diyas* are lit. These are placed in and around Indian homes to foster

▲ An artist paints clay idols in preparation for the Hindu festival of Divali at a workshop in Calcutta, India. Divali is celebrated by Hindus all over India.

spiritual illumination. The name *Divali* actually comes from a word meaning "a row of lights" in the ancient Indian language of Sanskrit.

All of these preparations have as their end goal the rightful welcome of Hindu gods and goddesses into the home for Divali, particularly Lakshmi. Although there are many gods that could be honored in different Hindu homes throughout Asia, there are just a few to whom large numbers of people pay tribute. These vary by region: Children in northern India will light the *diyas* with their parents to welcome King Rama back from exile, whereas households in southern India may retell the story of Lord Krishna defeating Narakasura, a ruthless, demonic king who tyrannically ruled over the heavens and the Earth.

A favorite story in western and southwestern India concerns a strange, smart, sometimes generous but always power-hungry king by the name of Bali. In the story, Vishnu, who has come back to Earth disguised as a dwarf, tricks Bali into giving up his power. Vishnu sends Bali to the underworld until peace is restored. Hindus in the southwestern Indian state of Kerala do not just celebrate Vishnu's victory, but also Bali's obedient spirit.

THE ARRIVAL OF HINDU DIVALI

After weeks of preparation Divali finally arrives. The smells of *kofta* curry, vegetables in sweet curry sauce; and *paneer makhani*, Indian cheeses simmered in a tomato sauce, fill the air. The scents of mouth-watering sweets such as *kadame kheer*, delicious hand-rolled cheese balls cooked in sugar syrup, waft from Hindu kitchens across the country. Multicolored drawings and paintings created by Hindus line the sidewalks of city streets and tiny villages alike. Businesses and homeowners decorate their freshly cleaned offices and abodes with lush displays of plants and flowers. Throngs of people stroll the streets and markets, dressed in new saris (flowing, wrapped dresses) and *dhotis* (draped skirts for men) made of traditional, brightly colored Indian textiles. It seems as if

A FEAST OF THE GODS

Hindu Indians make mountains of sweets in preparation for Divali. Hinduism emphasizes the role of food so much that it is sometimes called "the kitchen religion." *Prasada* (meaning mercy) is the name of any food that is offered to God. It is an important part of worship. Hindus believe that the consciousness of the cook enters the food and affects the person who eats it. Therefore food that has been prepared with devotion will bring greater spirituality to the eater. Food that has been on the altar is particularly sacred. It is usually distributed to worshippers during or after a religious ceremony.

all of India is out socializing, wearing glittering jewelry, visiting friends and relatives, and attending public parties and parades. The nights are radiant with the glow of thousands of lights as well as the sights and sounds of laughing children and exploding fireworks.

Whereas in most areas of the United States and many other Western countries it is illegal for people to set off their own fireworks, until recently in India anyone could set off fireworks–and, on the third day of Divali, that is exactly what they did. The result was an all-night party with both the street and sky ablaze with *diyas*, fireworks, and electric lights. However, due to the many firework-related injuries that have occurred over the years, modern regulations now prohibit fireworks use in India. Though this might have taken away from the spectacle of the holiday, it has not dulled the festive tone of the celebration or the **reverence** for Lakshmi and all that she symbolizes.

The fourth day of Divali, the official new year, is called Annakut (*ann* means food; *kut* means mountain) or Govardhan Puja in many of the central and northeastern Indian states. Both names refer to the legend of Krishna holding up the mountain to save the creatures of the region.

▲ Hindus celebrate Divali with sparklers in Allahabad, India.

In some states of India, such as Uttar Pradesh, Bihar, and Madhya Pradesh, people commemorate Lord Krishna's feat by building hillocks of cow dung. They decorate them with flowers and then offer prayers to them. In other areas, a huge array of vegetarian dishes is offered to the deities. It is traditional to place the dishes on tiers or steps in front of statues of the deities, with a mound of cooked rice in the middle to represent Mount Govardhana. Worshippers sing about the food, chanting the names of the dishes in a poetic, rhythmic way and praying for the food to be accepted. Everyone enjoys the food that

HOLIDAY BUSINESS

The third day of Divali is considered a good time to start a new business or move into a new home. In some regions, this is the day that account books are presented to Lakshmi and the elephant-headed god, Ganesh, for blessing. In northern India, businesspeople and accountants begin their financial new year on the fourth day of Divali.

▲ A special prayer is performed at a temple on the occasion of Divali in Mumbai, India.

has been blessed and offered to God. In the end the remaining food gets distributed evenly for everyone to take home.

Many Indians are vegetarian, but during religious holidays such as Govardhan Puja, all Hindus eat only vegetarian food. They even avoid dairy products such as eggs and milk. Instead, they feast on an Indian rice pudding called *kheer*, which can be made without eggs and is cooked with crushed cardamom seeds, almonds, pistachio nuts, and raisins. This dish is usually accompanied by spicy *urid lentil vada* (lentil fritters). Such a dish might be made as a Govardhan Puja offering to Krishna, or served on one of the five days of Divali.

SIKH DIVALI IN INDIA

Sikhism is a religion that differs from both Hinduism and Islam but retains traits of each. It was founded by a man known as Guru Nanak in 1469. The central elements of Sikhism are the emphasis on good works and moral acts and the absence of rituals frequently associated with Hinduism and other religions. The path to the one god of the Sikh comes through meditation, deep reflection, and prayer, as well as study of the sacred Sikh text called the Granth Sahib.

For Sikhs, Divali is a time to remember the release of an important spiritual teacher, Hargobind, from imprisonment by a Mughal emperor during the 17th century. The Mughals were a Muslim dynasty that ruled northern India and other parts of southern Asia for close to two centuries. Hargobind refused to accept his freedom until the 52 Hindu princes imprisoned with him were also released. Eventually the Mughal emperor granted his wish. To commemorate this event, Sikhs light lamps in the Golden Temple, their principal house of worship and pilgrimage site located in the city of Amritsar in the northwest part of India. This temple, already beautiful during daylight, looks magical when illuminated by the lights of Divali.

JAIN DIVALI IN INDIA

More than 3 million Jains who live throughout India also observe Divali. Jainism is a religion believed to be related to both Hinduism and Buddhism, but with many separate beliefs as well. For example, the gods Rama and Krishna have additional characteristics in Jainism that they do not have in Hinduism, such as holiness and nonviolence. For Jains, Divali honors the historic founder of their religion, Vardhmana Mahavira, who taught of nonviolence and compassion. They believe that it was during Divali when Mahavira achieved a state of nirvana, or total enlightenment, that freed him from his earthly body and the eternal cycle of birth and death. On the evening before the first day of Divali, Jains pray to Mahavira at midnight. The next day they read from their holy scriptures, including the sayings and teachings of Vardhamana Mahavira. Along with these readings comes an intensive fast, which is a direct contrast to the Hindu tradition of feasting during Divali. Like Indian Hindus, the Jains also light up their homes for Divali with *diyas*. However, they do so because they believe that when Mahavira died, he took with him the light of divine knowledge. Therefore, their *diyas* represent the desire to rekindle the spirit of his wisdom.

▪ Ashura in India

For Shii Muslims, the 10th day of Muharram, Ashura, is a day of sorrow. To remember the sufferings of Hussein and his troops at the hands of the Sunnis, as well as to atone for their sins, some Shii men will inflict wounds on their bodies with sharp knives. More commonly, Shii men will strike their chests in hard, rhythmic beats while chanting. During this period of mourning, Shii women take off all jewelry and the men dress in black and recite incidents from the Battle of Karbala. Wrestlers and dancers recreate scenes from the battle that took Hussein's life. When one takes a cold drink at any point in Ashura, he or she must be mindful to remember the thirst that Hussein and his followers had to endure in captivity. In India, the Shii people will parade replicas of Hussein's tomb, called *tazias*, in long, meandering processions through the streets. Some parts of India such as Hyderabad and Lucknow are famous for their elaborately decorated tombs. Though Shii Muslims make up only 2 percent of the Muslim population of India, these dramatic, often meticulously staged rituals of Ashura make them a highly visible presence during the month of Muharram.

▪ Divali in Nepal

Nepal is the only Hindu kingdom in the world and thus places particular emphasis on its Divali celebrations. In addition to the bright lights, fireworks, and feasts traditionally associated with Divali, Nepalese Hindus place special meaning on the various days of the celebration. For instance, a different animal is worshipped each day, including crows, dogs, cows, and oxen. Each animal is associated with a different deity. The fourth day is especially devoted to Yama, the Hindu god of death. People recite prayers to him in hopes for a long and healthy life. The fifth and final day of Divali is called Bhai Tika. Similar to the Brother's Day, siblings put the *tika* (a design made of colored powder) on each other's foreheads and a *mala* (a necklace of woven flowers) around each other's necks. They then exchange wishes for a prosperous new year. This ritual is timed to happen at the exact same moment all over the country.

▲ A Nepalese woman feeds a cow, which is holy for Hindus, during Divali in Katmandu, Nepal.

■ Divali in Singapore

In Singapore, where 7.4 percent of the population is of Indian descent and 5.2 percent are Hindu, families believe that the *diyas* in their homes will guide the souls of their departed loved ones back to visit them. Although Hindus make up only a small percentage of the population, Divali is a large-scale festival celebrated throughout the country. In the cities, those neighborhoods with large Indian populations decorate their streets with garlands and lighted archways. Since many of these cities are dense with high-rise towers and clustered apartment buildings, people will gather in open areas such as parks to light sparklers and other small fireworks. The local Hindu temple is also a popular gathering spot, both in the daytime and in the evening, for the exchange of new year's greetings and the offering of prayers.

■ Divali in Sri Lanka

In Sri Lanka, Divali celebrations are more subdued than in other places. The mood is solemn and reflective, without the singing, dancing, firecrackers, and games that characteristically mark the holiday. However, there are some specific traditions Sri Lankan Hindus maintain, such as illuminating their homes and streets, making figures known as *misiri* out of crystallized sugar, and crafting and exchanging enamel toys. On the last day of Divali families share in a large meal including vegetable curries and sweets made with coconut milk and honey.

 TEXT-DEPENDENT QUESTIONS

1: How many days is the Chinese New Year?

2: Name one way that Indian Hindus prepare for Divali.

3: What are *misiri*?

 RESEARCH PROJECTS

1: Research the Chinese New Year, including its history, celebrations, and observations outside of China. Write a brief overview of the holiday, including how it differs from the religious new year's festivals of Asia.

2: Research more about either Sikhism of Jainism. Write a brief report that includes information about the religion's history, scriptures or sacred texts, key figures or spiritual leaders, and contemporary practices.

Celebrating in the Middle East

n the Middle East, the two main religious new year's observances are Rosh Hashanah, celebrated by Jews, and Al-Hijra, observed by Muslims. The significance of these celebrations is deeply religious. They are as much about looking back into each

WORDS TO UNDERSTAND

Martyrdom: Suffering or death inflicted as the result of a person remaining true to a cause, especially a religious cause.

Monotheism: The belief in the supremacy of one god (as opposed to many) that began with Judaism more than 4,000 years ago and also includes the major religions of Islam and Christianity.

Palestinians: People who speak Arabic and who are originally from or had family in Palestine.

Passion play: The reenactment or retelling of a central religious experience or event for a religious people.

Penitence: Feeling of regret or sadness for wrongs or offenses a person has committed.

◀ Al-Hijra, the Islamic new year's holiday, marks the time that the prophet Muhammad was forced to flee from Mecca to the town of Yathrib (later renamed Medina, which means "City of the Prophet"), where he formed the first Islamic state.

community's rich history as they are about looking forward to the coming year. For both Jews and Muslims, the new year is a period of deep self-reflection and a time to make amends to loved ones and to God. Repentance is a common theme for both faiths during this month.

For the Jews of Israel, Rosh Hashanah is one of the most important religious celebrations of the year. For most Muslims in the Middle East, Al-Hijra is the day to remember the flight of Muhammad from Mecca to present day Medina in 622, which marks the first year of the Muslim calendar. Unlike many other Muslim holidays, there are few specific customs or rituals associated with Al-Hijra in most countries where Muslims live. It is a time to recount Muhammad's flight, look back over the past year, and prepare for the next.

Throughout the Middle East and parts of Africa, the morning of Al-Hijra does not make it immediately obvious that a new year is beginning. There are no fireworks displays, singing in the streets, or long parades associated with the Islamic new year. People do not light sparklers or candles like they do on the nights of Rosh Hashanah and Divali. In fact, on the morning of Al-Hijra the streets of Middle Eastern cities generally resemble "business as usual," although in some countries shops will close down for the day.

In Middle Eastern countries, especially those with large Sunni majorities, Al-Hijra is a time of personal reflection rather than outward celebration. It is a chance to resolve to become a better person and a better Muslim in the coming year. In this way it is much like other religious and civil new year's observances around the globe. However, it is also a day with a rich historical focus. Many Muslims will go to their mosques to hear the story of Prophet Muhammad's hijra from Mecca to present-day Medina. This event marks the period when Islam gelled as a religion. While a visit to the mosque is encouraged throughout Islam on this day, it is not mandatory. Families often choose to remain at home, where parents sit down with their children to discuss Muhammad's hijra and encourage them to think about how his emigration allowed for the birth of Islam.

A common aspect of both Rosh Hashanah observances and some of those of Al-Hijra is the importance of sweet foods. These represent the hopes that the new year will be free of bitterness and ill will. A more important linkage between these two faiths at this time of the year is a strong and solemn bond with their respective holy books. Even Jews and Muslims who do not actively practice religion on a daily basis still recount the histories, legends, and mythologies of their sacred texts. It is an important way of giving their children and other loved ones an understanding of their place on Earth as glimpsed through the workings of their faith.

■ Religions of the Middle East

THE TWO MAJOR MUSLIM SECTS: SHIIS AND SUNNIS

Close to 90 percent of the people who live in the Middle East today are Muslim. However, within this broad religious term there is a great variety of belief and practice, just as there is with different branches of Christianity and Judaism. Muslims are largely divided between Sunni and Shii sects, although there are numerous other branches of Islam that are connected to these two major groups. Sunni Muslims make up 85 to 90 percent of all Muslims around the world, mostly concentrated in Egypt, Turkey, Syria, Pakistan, and Saudi Arabia. Shii Muslims, on the other hand, are more populous in Iraq and Iran.

In some Middle Eastern countries there are tensions between Shii and Sunni Muslims, while in other regions there is relative harmony. In Iraq there has long been resentment on the part of the Shiis regarding Sunni rule, especially when Saddam Hussein, a Sunni, was in power (he was president of Iraq from 1979 to 2003).

CHRISTIANS AND JEWS

It is important to remember that in this largely Muslim region there are also Christian and Jewish communities, though they are comparatively small in number. In fact, these three major religions–Christianity, Islam, and Judaism–originated in the Middle East, and they all recognize the same ancestor, Abraham. For this reason, these religions are often referred to as the Abrahamic religions. All share the belief that there is only one God, who is the creator of the universe. This belief is known as monotheism.

COEXISTENCE IN AND AROUND ISRAEL

Approximately 14 million people around the world are Jewish, with the majority living in North America and Israel. The Jews have considered the land of Israel their home for more than 150 years. Ever since Jews began to move from the Diaspora back to Israel, they have fought with existing Muslim populations. This has been especially true in the years following World War II to the present. It has resulted in heavy bloodshed and great loss of life on both sides. By reclaiming what King David declared was their capital, the Jews moved Muslim Palestinians off land that they had lived on for many years, thus dividing the region into bitterly contested areas.

◀ A woman holds her child as she prays at the Western Wall, Judaism's holiest site, in Jerusalem's Old City.

JERUSALEM: MOST SACRED OF CITIES

Jerusalem, the capital of Israel (which became a Jewish state in 1948), is one of the holiest cities in the world for Jews, Muslims, and Christians. For Jews, it is tied to the reign of the great King David, who declared it the capital of his kingdom in 1000 B.C.E. For Christians, it is the place where Jesus was crucified, buried, and resurrected. For Muslims, it is the site of the Al-Aqsa Mosque, one of Islam's holiest shrines after the Kaaba in Mecca. At the center of the mosque is the Dome of the Rock, which has religious meaning for Muslims, Jews, and Christians. For Muslims, it is the place where Muhammad ascended into heaven. For Jews and Christians, it is the altar where Abraham was about to sacrifice his first-born son. Today in Israel, a country that measures 8,000 square miles and has a population of more than 8.5 million people, 75 percent of Israelis (around 6.4 million) are Jewish. Most of the remaining citizens are Muslim. However, from ancient times until today, the land that is now Israel has been fought over, occupied, and ruled by Muslims, Christians, and Jews alike in numerous power struggles of various lengths. Since 1948 it has been a place of great conflict and bloodshed between Jews and Muslims from neighboring Palestine and other Muslim territories.

◀ Muslim children remove their shoes before entering the Al-Aqsa Mosque compound for prayer, in Jerusalem, one of Islam's most holy sites.

After 1948 many Jews who had lived in various parts of the Middle East moved in large numbers to the new Jewish State of Israel. They were often forced to leave other Middle Eastern countries under direct threat of their Islamic governments. At the same time, Muslims who already lived in Israel were angry at being removed from lands they considered rightfully theirs. They also felt discriminated against because of their faith. Such sentiments continue to this day. In the midst of this tension, and partly because of it, adherence to the orthodox Jewish and Islamic beliefs and traditions is often unbending and impassioned. It is within this volatile environment that these two historically connected and yet very distinct religious groups practice their faith and celebrate their holidays.

◼ Ashura in Iraq

Shii men often reenact through passion plays the events that led up to the death of Imam Hussein on Ashura, 10 days after Al-Hijra. In many parts of Iran, which is 89 percent Shii, men and women wear black–the color of mourning–and the men beat their chests rhythmically with fists or iron chains in order to feel Hussein's pain and remember his martyrdom. (Some current Shii leaders discourage self-flagellation because they believe it gives non-Muslims the wrong image, or perception, of Shii Muslims. On this day they encourage the mourners to give blood at a blood bank instead.) Shii women also wail loudly in remembrance of him. Hauntingly beautiful processions include children carrying a cradle as a reminder of Hussein's child, who was killed in front of his father after Hussein demanded water from his captors. These processions are often led by a white horse without a rider to symbolize the horse that was left without a master when Hussein died.

In Iraq, especially in Karbala where Imam Hussein was killed, Ashura holds great significance for the Shiis. Under Saddam Hussein, a dictator who ruled Iraq from 1979 to 2003, traditional pilgrimages to Karbala on Ashura as well as the reenactments of Imam Hussein's death were restricted or banned outright for several years. Since most Shiis view Ashura as a symbol of the fight against tyranny and oppression, the former dictator of Iraq saw their observances as a possible threat to his rule. Shii Muslims have only recently begun to observe Ashura again after Saddam Hussein was removed from power and later executed. In 2004, the year after he was removed, more than 1 million Shiis traveled to Karbala for Ashura. This proved to be dangerous considering the instability of the region and the high tensions between Shii and Sunni Muslims. More than 100 Shiis died and more were injured in bomb attacks, even though the area was highly fortified. This attack demonstrates Iraq's continued struggle for stability. In such a place, simply showing devotion through religious rituals can have tragic, life-threatening consequences.

■ Rosh Hashanah in Israel

At some point on the first day of Rosh Hashanah, Jews in Israel will go in search of a body of water in order to perform tashlik. This is the ritual in which people empty their pockets of bread crumbs, stones, or other small items and throw them into the water to symbolize casting away their sins. As much of the Israeli landscape is dry desert, finding a body of water can be quite difficult. In Jerusalem, people sometimes stand above swimming pools, water tanks, wells, or even their kitchen sinks during this ritual.

For several days leading up to the new year, preparations for Rosh Hashanah are noticeable everywhere in Israel. Stores hold extended hours and have special prices for honey, an important dipping ingredient for sweet foods traditionally eaten on Rosh Hashanah. In kitchens everywhere, families make and pray over loaves of challah bread. In Israel during the lead-up to Rosh Hashanah, fruits overflow in the outdoor markets, especially pomegranates. Pomegranates are believed to have the same

A CALL FOR ALL

Even those who cannot attend services because they are ill or too elderly to make it to the Rosh Hashanah service are supposed to hear the sound of the shofar–a sound thought to inspire awe as well as God's compassion. In hospitals, Jewish chaplains will go from room to room with a shofar so that Jewish patients can hear the sound and in this way take part in Rosh Hashanah.

number of seeds–613–as there are commandments in the Torah. In addition to pomegranates, apples dipped in honey are another popular fruit to eat at the onset of the new year.

Watch and listen to *selichot* prayers in Israel.

On the morning of the second day of Rosh Hashanah families return to their places of worship for a longer service. In fact, the Rosh Hashanah religious service can go on for up to five hours, and sometimes even longer. It is often the largest and best-attended service of the year. On the days of Rosh Hashanah it is customary for people to wear their finest clothes to temple. Many wear white as a sign of purity. During the services, some of the world's most polished choruses sing beautiful music in the synagogues of Israel. The melodies are often solemn, but they are also full of hope for the new year.

On the two days when Rosh Hashanah is celebrated, no work is permitted anywhere in Israel. Israeli television often runs a live broadcast of the *selichot* prayers recited by a congregation in a synagogue in Jerusalem. These prayers are prayers of **penitence** that are traditionally recited at this time of year. Different Jewish communities recite the prayers at special times of the day. Ashkenazi Jews, who are descended from Jewish communities in what is now France, Germany, and Eastern Europe, start the lengthy prayers at midnight of Rosh Hashanah. Sephardic Jews, who are descended from Jewish communities in Spain and Portugal and who spread to England, Greece, and North and South America, start them much earlier. They begin reciting on the morning

◀ Jews pray while performing *tashlik*, a Rosh Hashanah ritual for casting sins upon the waters, in the coastal city of Ashdod, Israel.

of the first day of Elul, say them every day in the month leading up to Rosh Hashanah, and continue to say them for the 10 additional days leading up to Yom Kippur. In Israel Sephardic Jews often live in their own communities and attend temples with architecture similar to Moorish-style mosques, usually colored in pastels. This influence is the result of Sephardic Jews having lived peacefully in Spain when it was under Islamic control from the eighth through the 11th centuries.

■ Al-Hijra in Saudi Arabia

While there are no fireworks or festivities on this first day of Al-Hijra, it is traditional in some places to clean homes and wear new clothes just as it is for the Hindu and Jewish new year. It is also a day to make resolutions for the coming year and to gather together to eat with extended family and friends. In Saudi Arabia, these family meals often include dishes in the colors green and white as representations of fertility and purity. To make sure they consume these lucky colors on this first day of the new year, Saudi

◀ Sweet foods, such as these Syrian pastries made with pistachio nuts and honey, are enjoyed during Al-Hijra.

families always drink glasses of milk and prepare a dish called *molokhia*, a nutritious soup made from a type of green plant known as mallow. In Saudi Arabia, businesses are closed for the day.

Al-Hijra in Syria

During Al-Hijra, Muslims in Syria and some Christians in the Middle East will often prepare a sweet wheat pudding called *asure* or *ashura*. It is believed to be the last food that Noah ate before his ark reached dry land. It is also believed that Noah made the pudding by gathering together all the foods left on the ark when its inhabitants were near starvation, waiting for the floods to recede. This dish, also referred to as "Noah's pudding," contains wheat, beans, dried fruits such as dates and raisins, and nuts. Other Syrian traditions for Al-Hijra include decorating the streets with lights and gathering friends and family together for gift exchanges.

TEXT-DEPENDENT QUESTIONS

1: What do Muslims remember on the day of Al-Hijra?

2: Where is the Dome of the Rock located?

3: What are the ingredients of "Noah's pudding"?

RESEARCH PROJECTS

1: Research the nearest mosque and synagogue to your hometown. Find out about their locations, their histories, and their current programs of prayer and worship. Write a brief report summarizing your findings.

2: Research various prayers and blessings of both the Jewish and Islamic traditions. Create a short anthology of these prayers, including information about the histories of their composition, when they are said, and any special prayer movements or positions.

Celebrating in North America

Despite the fact that North America is made up of countries that are predominantly Christian, with close to 80 percent of their populations identifying themselves as Protestant or Roman Catholic, the landscape includes millions of people of other faiths, including Hindus, Muslims, and Jews. The United States is a religiously diverse place largely because there is a written commitment to religious freedom in the U.S. Constitution. Similarly, Canada has a criminal code that prohibits expression of hatred against people identified by their race, color, religious, or ethnic origin. These guarantees

WORDS TO UNDERSTAND

Communism: A system of government in which the state controls the economy as well as all property or wealth of a country.

Convert: To accept new opinions or beliefs, especially religious viewpoints, or to change the opinions or beliefs of another person.

Holocaust: From Greek word for "sacrifice by fire," the deliberate killing of close to 6 million Jews (as well as gypsies, intellectuals, homosexuals, and political protesters) in Europe by the Nazis and their supporters, under the command of Adolf Hitler during World War II.

◄ A man blows a shofar to mark the Jewish new year. Rosh Hashanah and Yom Kippur are often referred to as the High Holy Days because they are the most sacred in the Jewish calendar.

to the freedom of worship and expression are powerful lures for people of different religious faiths, especially those faiths that are persecuted by governments in other parts of the world. They are a good part of the reason why, for example, so many Jewish communities have been motivated to immigrate here and put down roots outside of their homelands. Today there are more than 5 million Jews in the United States, almost as many as live in Israel. There are also approximately 390,000 Jews in Canada and 40,000 in Mexico, the fourth- and 14th-largest Jewish populations by country, respectively, in the world.

Another important draw for those of different religions, cultures, and nationalities to make new lives for themselves in North America is the opportunity for economic growth. In many countries of the world there are few jobs for a great number of people. When parents have children to feed and clothe, they will go to the place that allows them to best survive. This is what has often motivated individuals, families, and whole communities to immigrate to North America–the hope for a better life. This diversity has resulted in the addition of many unique skills and talents from all over the world, which in turn has served to strengthen the nation economically.

In the 20th century, especially after World War II, U.S. and Canadian laws allowed for larger groups of immigrants to come to North America to live and work permanently. At the same time, economic and religious suffering in other parts of the world such as Europe and Asia continue to make North America a promising destination.

■ Religion in North America

JUDAISM IN NORTH AMERICA

Although the United States Bill of Rights promises religious freedom to all, in immigration law there has been a bias, or favoritism, shown toward immigrants from European countries. This was especially true in the 19th and 20th centuries. It is why there was a visible Jewish community in the United States much earlier than any other religion, as during this time most Jews came to the United States from northern or eastern Europe. In Canada, the influx of Jewish émigrés was considerably less than in the United States, but still quite sizable. Many were enticed to settle there by job offers from the Canadian government to help build railways and other public works projects.

HINDUISM IN NORTH AMERICA

It was not until the Immigration Act of 1965 that the United States lifted a quota system limiting immigration from Asian countries. Canada, too, did not always have a lenient immigration policy for those of Asian descent, placing a tax on Chinese immigrants until 1923 and relocating many

Japanese immigrants in the years following World War II. Over time, the immigration policies in both the United States and Canada liberalized to allow the arrival of Asian immigrants from many places, including India. Before 1965, India had very little presence in the United States or Canada, and neither did its predominant religion, Hinduism. Today there are close to 1 million Hindus in the United States and more than 150,000 Hindus in Canada.

ISLAM IN NORTH AMERICA

The percentages of Muslims in the United States vary, and there are no solid statistics that organizations can agree upon. This is in part because of the political and religious tensions that arose from the terrorist attacks of September 11, 2001, making many Muslims especially reluctant to tell surveyors their religion. Several studies indicate that there are somewhere between 3 and 6 million Muslims in North America, some of them from Africa, Asia, or the Middle East. Another source of statistical confusion is that many Muslims in the United States did not emigrate from another country but are African Americans who were born into American Muslim families or **converted**.

Muslims make up 3 percent of the Canadian population with over 1 million in number. This is significantly larger than the Canadian Jewish population. Unlike the United States where large numbers of Muslims are African American converts or were born in the United Sates, most Canadian Muslims have come from Muslim countries around the world, the majority of them since 1973. The largest population of Muslims in Canada lives in the capital Ottawa, where it is common to see women dressed in traditional Muslim clothing.

THE CHALLENGE OF MAINTAINING RELIGIOUS OBSERVANCES

Perhaps the biggest issue for many of the diaspora communities that celebrate their new years and other important religious days in North America is finding a way to pass on their religious customs and celebrations to their children. For some this problem is solved by continuing to observe holidays and not allowing the rites and rituals associated with them to die out. They may invite members of their city or town to celebrate with them, and in this way gain formal recognition for their holidays from city councils and town officials. Such recognition acknowledges the importance of their rites, traditions, and customs within their adopted homelands.

For those who are used to living in countries dominated by one religion, settling in North America requires adjusting to the interaction of numerous different religions on a daily basis. Often it is much harder to feel at home in a particular culture or religion in such an environment. To compensate for this, minority religious communities band together to teach their children some of the things they are missing by being away from their native landscape. For example, in the United

States Hindu children often go to weekly classes to learn what they might have picked up through everyday living in South Asia, such as language, manners, customs, and culinary traditions. Muslim Americans do something similar by bringing together African, South Asian, and Middle Eastern Muslim children in school-type environments to discuss how their cultures differ from U.S. culture. When the time for new year's celebrations comes–be it in September, November, or February–families are especially aware of their new environment as they work to preserve old traditions.

Rosh Hashanah in North America

Judaism is the most observed non-Christian religion in most parts of North America today, and the official recognition of major Jewish observances is testament to that visibility. For instance, the dates of Rosh Hashanah are printed on many calendars in the United States. Some colleges and universities officially state that Jewish students are not expected to attend class on Rosh Hashanah and should be allowed to make up tests and other work. (Most extend this policy to students of other faiths as well.) While Jews in North America–especially those who immigrated as adults after years in their native land or who live in communities with few Jews–may feel a sense of isolation while celebrating the major holidays, they also have a long, historic tradition in North America that can make adjustment easier.

A small number of Jews have lived in North America since the early 1700s and fought alongside Christians in the 1776 American Revolution. The early Jews were mostly Sephardic (coming from Spain and Portugal) and settled in eastern cities such as New York. A second group that came in the 19th century was mostly Ashkenazi (from Germany). The Ashkenazi Jews were usually well-educated and as they came in greater numbers they began to establish synagogues in urban areas where other Jews lived and worked. These Jews were often shop owners. They led more secular lives than Sephardic Jews but still maintained their own places of worship and sense of community and established important Jewish fraternal organizations that still exist today.

It was during the end of the 19th century and beginning of the 20th century in Eastern Europe that Jews became the target of pogroms, or violent anti-Jewish uprisings, that spurred large scale immigration to other countries. Between the 1880s and 1930s, Jews arrived in large numbers in the United States and in smaller numbers in Canada to escape persecution. The next great wave of Jewish immigration to both the United States and Canada was during and after the Holocaust.

▲ A rabbi uses a *yad*, popularly known as a Torah pointer, to follow the text on the parchment Torah scrolls for a Rosh Hashanah service in Weldon, North Carolina.

When the Romans destroyed Jewish temples in ancient Jerusalem, making temple worship impossible, Jews turned to rabbis for guidance. Out of necessity they began to believe that the places where they worshipped were less important than simply keeping their faith. This belief has stayed with the Jews as a people to the present day. It has helped them cope with having to live scattered around the globe due to persecution and oppression from Christians and Muslims in the Middle Ages all the way through Nazi Germany in modern times. They have been forced to focus on rules and rituals of their faith set down over different times in different places. This means that wherever Jews settle, they often stay true to the traditions of the branch of Judaism they follow.

Not surprisingly then, the traditions, religious ceremonies, and customs of Rosh Hashanah in North America are very similar to those of Rosh Hashanah in Israel, or anywhere else on the planet where Jews have settled. If there are differences, they are usually based on the different branches of Judaism, just as they are in Israel—they are rarely based on the differences of the countries in which the holiday is being celebrated. For example, Reform Jews who celebrate Rosh Hashanah for only one day instead of the two will do so anywhere in the world, living according to their tradition and not that of the surrounding culture.

Jews in the Diaspora (the world outside the Holy Land of antiquity), including North America, might live in overwhelmingly Christian communities with such small Jewish populations that no synagogue exists. For Jews in towns and rural areas without a temple, families often establish places of worship in basements of Christian churches or other rented spaces. These communities may also host a rabbi from the closest city for High Holy Day services such as those for Rosh Hashanah. Perhaps because of all they have sacrificed to get here, many Jews in North America celebrate their holidays more fervently than they would if they lived in Israel where Judaism is the main religion. This is especially true if they came from countries such as Russia that prohibited or severely reduced all religious ceremonies during the Soviet years under communism.

ROSH HASHANAH IN CANADA

Rosh Hashanah celebrations in Canada bear many similarities to those that take place in the United States. As Jewish populations in Canada are more concentrated in the urban areas of Vancouver, Toronto, and Montreal, there are opportunities for widespread community gatherings, both within

▲ The traditional Ashkenazi Jewish holiday dessert of *taiglach* waits to be devoured. *Taiglach*, a mound of baked dough balls mixed with candied cherries and drenched with honey and sugar, is eaten during Rosh Hashanah.

individual synagogues and through the collaboration of different congregations. As in the United States, shared meals such as bagel breakfasts or potluck dinners are a popular way of getting people together to meet, discuss, and pray for a prosperous new year. In cultural centers such as Vancouver, many synagogues will organize lectures, film screenings, and dance performances informed by the Jewish experience and inspired by the passage of Rosh Hashanah. Rabbis may visit other synagogues to guide meditation sessions or lead prayer groups. With this practice, members of the religious communities and spiritual leaders alike are mutually renewed by each other's presence. They give each other a fresh perspective with which to begin the new year.

ROSH HASHANAH IN THE UNITED STATES

Despite the universal nature of Rosh Hashanah, certain traditions and customs of the holiday are tied to specific places in both the United States and Canada. In the United States, for instance, Rosh Hashanah often falls on or near Labor Day. Since this secular holiday is often a popular time to visit the beach before the cool days of autumn arrive, some Jews will do this in addition to attending Rosh Hashanah services. The result is a swell in the attendance of congregations in resort beach communities such as the Hamptons outside of New York City. In other American cities, Rosh Hashanah often takes the form of a community event as much as a religious holiday, as synagogues organize potluck dinners, lectures, and group outings such as hikes or historical tours of the area. One community in Falls Village, Connecticut, even puts together a voluntary retreat for its members, complete with yoga classes and canoe trips. Such events are seen as a way to find the peace and quiet necessary to this most reflective time of year.

Divali in North America

In the 1970s Hindus began arriving in the United States in greater numbers. At that time there were almost no Hindu temples in North America. One of the few places that Hindus could go to worship were the Krishna temples of the Hare Krishna movement. Krishna Hinduism is a form of Hinduism that stresses chanting, movement, and singing the name of Krishna, as well as highly ritualized devotions to Krishna. Krishna worshippers have been chanting in India for 400 years. They do not exclude anyone from worship, and they exalt the love of God over human-made rules. The Hare Krishna movement began in the United States in the 1960s. Hare Krishnas were known in the 1960s and 1970s for their evangelizing, singing, and offering sweets and literature to anyone who passed by. At the time, they were the prominent face of Hinduism in North America. Youthful adherents in saffron robes were a common sight in airports and major cities around the United States. During the tumultuous 1960s they converted many questioning young adults–often to the dismay of their Christian parents. Hindu immigration to Canada began in earnest toward the end of the British Empire at the turn of the 20th century as Hindus from crown territories such as India were drawn to the former British possession by economic prospects.

Devotees of Krishna filled a very important role for newly arriving Hindus. Because Hare Krishnas had temples in major cities where Hindu immigrants were settling, such as Dallas, Denver, Chicago, and Los Angeles, they often served as a place for immigrants to gather before forming their own places of worship. Equally as important, they provided a place for Hindu immigrants to celebrate holidays such as Divali when they were feeling homesick for their native India.

In the early years after the 1965 Immigration Act in the 1960s and 1970s, Hindus mostly celebrated Divali and other major Hindu festivals by gathering with a few Hindu families in their homes, lighting the traditional *diyas*, worshipping, and sharing food. While the celebration used to last only one or two days, Divali can now last up to five days in North America just as it does in India.

DIVALI IN CANADA

Canadian prime ministers have been helping ring in the Hindu new year for several years now. In Ottawa Prime Minister Justin Trudeau marked the Divali New Year in 2015 by visiting a Hindu temple and taking the opportunity to praise Canada for its commitment to diversity.

In places in Canada without such widespread public recognition, Hindus still find ways to gather and make the holiday meaningful, whether by feasting together in a neighbor's home or reserving a local school gymnasium, storefront mall, or city warehouse in order to pray to their gods for prosperity and celebrate the victory of good over evil. There are around 500,000 practicing Hindus in Canada. Their Divali traditions keep with those from around the world, including the establishment of a prayer room, or puja,

A GROWING HINDU PRESENCE

In 1977 there was only one Hindu temple that had been built from the ground up in the United States, the Ganesha Temple in Queens, New York. Today there are hundreds around the country, both in large cities like New York and Chicago and smaller ones such as Nashville.

▲ A boy lights candles for the Hindu festival of Divali at his home. Divali marks the start of the Hindu new year and the coming of winter. "We say, 'God bless everybody.' We don't just pray for ourselves," said the young man's father.

in their homes and the bathing of coins in milk—the substance from which Lakshmi was born—as part of the ceremony to welcome the goddess into their homes on Lakshmi Puja.

DIVALI IN THE UNITED STATES

In 2009, Barack Obama became the first U.S. president to light the *diya* candle. In Queens, New York, trees on 74th Street in the Jackson Heights neighborhood are lighted

Check out scenes from an American Divali celebration.

on Divali and stay lit through the Muslim holiday of Eid, Christian Christmas, Jewish Hanukkah, and the civil new year that is generally celebrated by everyone regardless of religious background. While many Hindus have emigrated from India, a large number have come from Guyana and Trinidad and Tobago, bringing their Caribbean-inflected Divali traditions with them to mix with those of the existing U.S. Hindu population.

In Houston, Texas, where 150,000 Indian-Americans live, Divali has been celebrated in City Hall since 2004. Every year the mayor inaugurates the holiday and the whole community is invited to ceremonies provided by the many Hindu temples. Divali bazaars feature *rangoli* contests for children, a health fair, live entertainment, and specialty vendors selling books, jewelry, and other things.

Al-Hijra in North America

When Syrian and Lebanese Muslim immigrants came to the United States more than 100 years ago, there was already a very small Muslim community made up of former slaves who had retained their religious beliefs after being forcibly taken from West Africa. While little study has been done of these early Muslims in North America, it is known that nearly 10 percent of African slaves were Muslim. During their years of toiling on U.S. soil, many were converted to Christianity, though some continued to practice Islam and did so until being freed in the late 19th century.

Around this time Syrian Muslims and Christians came to America for its economic opportunity. Most intended to return home after making money. But like many immigrants before and after them, most were thrilled when they experienced the freedoms democracy promised such as equal opportunity and individual liberty. Consequently, some did not return to the Middle East. These immigrants encouraged others from their homeland to come join them. Early Muslims were often peddlers, selling goods in rural areas where farmers and others in the community lived far away from stores. In order to practice their religion in a country without mosques, they would rotate going to houses for regular prayers. One Muslim community in Cedar Rapids, Iowa, had its first imam, or prayer leader, in 1929. By 1936 it had raised enough money to build a temple. Cedar Rapids was to be an important place for early Muslim pioneers, who taught American-born Muslims to speak Arabic and study the Quran. In 1952 Cedar Rapids's Abdullah Igram helped to form the Federation of Islamic Associations in order to fight negative Muslim stereotypes after being denied the right to select his religion as "Islam" when registering for service in World War II.

Early in the 20th century in Detroit, Michigan, Henry Ford offered Muslims five dollars a day to work for Ford Motor Company (Ford's focus on Muslims had partly to do with his notorious dislike of Jews and unions). Muslims came to work for Ford in Dearborn, Michigan. In recent years, especially after the opening up of immigration laws in 1965, the population of Muslims in Dearborn has swelled; an estimated 40 percent of its 94,000 residents identify as Muslim. Southeastern Michigan has a population of about 300,000 Muslims, many of Lebanese and Iraqi descent.

In addition, this Detroit group has many large groups of African Americans who converted, or whose parents converted, to Islam throughout the 20th century and whose most vocal leaders included Elijah Muhammad and Malcolm X. Many of the

ISLAM ON THE PLAINS

Syrian Muslim peddlers ended up settling in North Dakota in the 1920s, numbering between 35 and 40 families. In 1920 one of the first mosques in the United States was built in Ross, North Dakota. Another early mosque was built in Highland Park, Michigan, in 1915, and another in Michigan City, Indiana, in 1925. This is the oldest still in use today.

converts were southern black Christians searching for a new identity after moving from the South to the North to find jobs. They often did not feel that Christianity's white portrayal of Jesus spoke to them. As they learned about their Muslim African heritage through the teachings of dynamic Muslims, they converted in large numbers. Today nearly three-fourths of Muslims in the United States are African American.

More and more Muslims have come in recent years from Asia and the Middle East to North America. Arab imams and leaders in the United States and Canada often report the need to spend a large amount of time educating North Americans about Islam and its many peaceful principles, as well as its belief in the equality of races. This is important if they are to counter negative media images that consistently equate Islam with radical Islamic terrorist groups. Since 9/11, more than half of Canadian Muslims say they have been the target of discrimination and feel they have to work hard to address stereotypes.

Al-Hijra is celebrated quietly by diaspora Muslims in the United States and Canada. Muslims get together and reflect on the past year and discuss how they want to proceed in the new one. They might exchange gifts or ask each other's forgiveness for wrongdoing during the year as well as share a meal. For some Muslims the day reminds them of financial responsibilities to those less fortunate. Fathers and mothers communicate to their children that this is the day that begins the Muslim calendar, relating the story of Muhammad's flight from Mecca. Thus, within the complicated

 Many North American Muslims, such as this family, observe Al-Hijra with a shared meal.

cultural, social, and political environments of contemporary North America, Muslims find ways to continue to celebrate their religious traditions.

TEXT-DEPENDENT QUESTIONS

1: Approximately how many Jews are there in Canada?

2: In what New York neighborhood are trees lighted on Divali?

3: How is Al-Hijra celebrated by diaspora Muslims in the United States and Canada?

RESEARCH PROJECTS

1: Research the history of the Middle Eastern population in Michigan, specifically the Detroit metropolitan area. Write a brief report including information about when various groups settled, their reasons for immigrating, their contributions to the local community, and significant challenges they might have faced or are currently facing.

2: Research some key moments in the history of Hinduism in the United States, including the arrival of Anandibai Joshi, Swami Vivekananda's address to the World's Parliament of Religions in Chicago, the wave of immigration in the 1960s, and other significant events. Create a timeline of these events with brief annotations.

▲ Middle Eastern bakeries, such as this one in Dearborn, Michigan, do a brisk business during Al-Hijra.

Celebrating in Oceania

The region of Oceania is made up of many island countries scattered across the Pacific Ocean, primarily in the Southern Hemisphere. Australia, the largest of these islands, together with New Zealand, makes up the part of Oceania identified as Australasia. Of the other parts of Oceania, Micronesia, Melanesia, and Polynesia, Polynesia is most familiar to North Americans because it includes the U.S. state of Hawaii. Many of the islands of Oceania reflect great cultural diversity. The largest number of people in Hawaii are of Asian ancestry, followed by Native Hawaiians. The islands are also home to people of German, Irish, Portuguese, Puerto Rican, African, Italian, Mexican, French, and British ancestry. There are also the Maori, an indigenous group with Polynesian roots that first settled New Zealand before 1300. They are the first known inhabitants of New Zealand.

New Zealand is an island country divided into two parts, South Island and North Island. The Maori live primarily on North Island. Their ancestors are believed to have come by canoe from Polynesia to New Zealand. Today the Maori make up close to 15 percent of the country's population and number around 600,000.

WORDS TO UNDERSTAND

Ancestry: **The origins of a person's family or ethnicity.**
Australasia: **A region in Oceania that includes Australia and New Zealand.**
Resurgence: **A renewal of activity or interest in something.**

◄ **Maori women dance in celebration of the new year.**

◀ A Maori man dances with traditionally tattooed face and in traditional dress.

■ Matariki in Taranaki, New Zealand

In Taranaki, on the west coast of the North Island of New Zealand, the elders watch for Matariki. While waiting, they make a clay oven and place food inside to cook. When the stars finally rise, they weep and tell the stars the names of those they have lost during the year. Then they uncover the oven so that the food will rise and give strength to the stars. They sometimes do this while singing a traditional Matariki song.

In the 1970s, New Zealand artists began to rediscover their ancestor's tradition of creating and flying kites. Some made new kites based on ancient designs, while others created paintings and sculptures inspired by the kites. This **resurgence** of interest has continued to the present day. They are once again a part of Matariki celebrations with all of their symbolic and spiritual meanings. In the spirit of Maori inventiveness and creativity, hot air balloons and fireworks now accompany the soaring kites. At "The Great Matariki Vintage Car Balloon Race" in Hastings, New Zealand, you can choose to ride in one of the hot air balloons or jump into a vintage car and chase the balloons across the island, hoping to end up where they land.

Learn more about Maori kites.

> *He taonga tuku iho, ko te manu tukutuku, kua ngaro atu ke ki nga hau e wha, kua whakamiharo a tatou nei ngakau kia puta ake ki te whaiao, ki te ao marama.*
> *(A treasured kite lost to the winds brings much joy when found again.)*
> —Maori proverb

◀ Kite flying festivals, such as this one in a Tauranga, New Zealand park, are an increasingly popular way to celebrate Matariki.

Matariki in Taumarunui, New Zealand

In Taumarunui, a town in the central North Island of New Zealand, one current Matariki festivity is the Te Huapae O Matariki ("Matariki on the Horizon") Fashion Show. Conceived in 2002, this event brings together members of the local community to celebrate the ancient Maori art of weaving clothing from native plants, leaves, and other materials. Over the weekend-long event, visitors are treated to demonstrations, exhibitions, and runway shows of these garments. Additionally, teachers are on site to help those who want to try to make their own pieces and experience firsthand this indigenous tradition.

Matariki in Wairoa, New Zealand

Wairoa, located on the east coast of North Island, is known as the "Maori Heartland." It is fitting, then, that the town should have its own Matariki festival, opening with a dawn

CHASING KITES AND HOT AIR BALLOONS IN HASTINGS, NEW ZEALAND

As Maori have found a renewed interest in their culture, Matariki celebrations are once again becoming part of New Zealand life. A diverse crowd of 500 people came to the first Maori new year's celebration held in the year 2000 in the city of Hastings on the North Island. Three years later, the number of attendees tripled. Thanks in part to the Maori Language Commission and the New Zealand National Museum, the celebration has now spread to other locations in New Zealand such as Auckland, Taumarunui, and Wairoa. It also continues to evolve in ways that could never have been imagined by the early Maori. There is even a move to replace the Queen's Birthday holiday with Matariki!

MAKING MATARIKI A PROUD TRADITION FOR NEW ZEALAND

A lot of New Zealanders would like to see Matariki become a central celebration to offset the negativity associated with Waitangi Day. This is a day set aside to honor a treaty made between the Maori and the British. Because many Maori feel they were not granted the land rights that the treaty promised, they often use Waitangi Day as a chance to protest government policies.

ceremony during which viewers are treated to a spectacular view of the Matariki stars and proceeding through a week of concerts, fireworks, and parades. More than 100 art and craft vendors line the streets of the town during this week, selling everything from traditional Maori products such as woven garments, modern art pieces reinterpreting the indigenous culture, and contemporary photography documenting the current state of the Maori.

Another recent Matariki tradition is the annual Matariki Film Festival. This festival, which originated in Wairoa, brings together the films of several Maori and other indigenous filmmakers over four days of public screenings. Filmmakers from other countries are invited to view these rarely seen works and gain insight into the creation of indigenous artists. After making its debut in Wairoa, the festival travels to Auckland, Wellington, and Taumarunui in the days following Matariki. In this way other New Zealanders are able to see these productions of their country's developing film culture.

TEXT-DEPENDENT QUESTIONS

1: What U.S. state is located in Polynesia?

2: On which island of New Zealand do the Maori primarily live?

3: What is the Maori name for the Pleiades, and what does it mean?

 Maori warriors arrive in *wakas*, traditional war canoes.

RESEARCH PROJECTS

1: Research the musical traditions of the Maori, including traditional song forms; the role of chant, poetry, and dance; and contemporary artists and styles. Write a brief report summarizing your findings.

2: Research films either made by Maoris or featuring Maori-themed stories. Pretend you are a juror at the Matariki Film Festival, and put together a program of different films that you would want to show. Include information on the films' writers and directors, plotlines, and relationship to Maori culture.

Series Glossary

ancestors The direct family members of one who is deceased

aristocrat A member of a high social class, the nobility, or the ruling class

atonement The act of making up for sins so that they may be forgiven

ayatollah A major religious leader, scholar, and teacher in Shii Islam; the religious leader of Iran

colonial era A period of time between the 17th to 19th century when many countries of the Americas and Africa were colonized by Europeans.

colonize To travel to and settle in a foreign land that has already been settled by groups of people. To colonize can mean to take control of the indigenous groups already in the area or to wield power over them in order to control their human and physical resources.

commemorate To honor the memory of a person or event

commercialization The act of reorganizing or reworking something in order to extract profit from it

descendant One who comes from a specific ancestor

Eastern Orthodox Church The group of Christian churches that includes the Greek Orthodox, Russian Orthodox, and several other churches led by patriarchs in Istanbul (Constantinople), Jerusalem, Antioch, and Alexandria.

effigy A representation of someone or something, often used for mockery

equinox Either of the two times during each year when night and day are approximately the same length of time. The spring equinox typically falls around March 21 and the autumnal equinox around September 23.

fast To abstain from eating for a set period of time, or to eat at only prescribed times of the day as directed by religious custom or law.

feast day A day when a religious celebration occurs and an intricate feast is prepared and eaten.

firsthand From the original source; experienced in person

Five Pillars of Islam The five duties Muslims must observe: declaring that there is only one God and Muhammad is his prophet, praying five times a day, giving to charity, fasting during Ramadan, and making a pilgrimage to Mecca

foundation myth A story that describes the foundation of a nation in a way that inspires its people

Gregorian calendar The calendar in use through most of the world

hedonism The belief that pleasure is the sole good in life

Hindu A follower of Hinduism, the dominant religion of India

imam A leader; a scholar of Islam; the head of a mosque

indigenous Originating in or native to a specific region; often refers to living things such as people, animals, and plants

Islam The religious faith of Muslims. Muslims believe that Allah is the only God, and Muhammad was his prophet

Judaism A religion that developed among the ancient Hebrews. Followers of Judaism believe in one God and follow specific laws written in the Torah and the Talmud, and revealed to them by Moses.

Julian calendar Is named after Julius Caesar, a military leader and dictator of ancient Rome, who introduced it in 46 B.C.E. The Julian calendar has 365 days divided into 12 months, and begins on January 1. An extra day, or leap day, is added every four years (February 29) so that the years will average out to 365.242, which is quite close to the actual 365.242199 days of Earth's orbit.

lower realm In the Asian tradition, the place where the souls end up if their actions on Earth were not good

lunar Related to the Moon

martyr A person who willingly undergoes pain or death because of a strong belief or principle

masquerade A party to which people wear masks, and sometimes costumes or disguises

millennium 1,000 years

monarch A king or queen; a ruler who inherits the throne from a parent or other relative

monotheism The belief in the supremacy of one god (and not many) that began with Judaism more than 4,000 years ago and also includes the major religions of Islam and Christianity.

mosque An Islamic house of worship

mourning The expression of sorrow for the loss of a loved one, typically involving

movable feast A religious feast day that occurs on a different day every year

Muhammad The prophet to whom God revealed the Quran, considered the final prophet of Islam

mullah A clergyman who is an expert on the Quran and Islamic religious matters

Muslim A person who follows the Islamic religion

New Testament The books of the Bible that were written after the birth of Christ

New World A term used to describe the Americas from the point of view of the Western Europeans (especially those from France, England, Portugal, and Spain) who colonized and settled what is today North and South America.

offering Donation of food or money given in the name of a deity or God

Old Testament The Christian term for the Hebrew Scriptures of the Bible, written before the birth of Christ

oral tradition Stories told aloud, rather than written, as a way to pass down history

pagan Originally, someone in ancient Europe who lived in the countryside; a person or group that does not believe in one god, but often believes in many gods that are closely connected to nature and the natural world

pageantry Spectacle, elaborate display

parody Imitation of something, exaggerated for comic effect—for example, a parody of science fiction movies.

patria Fatherland; nation; homeland

peasant People who farm land that usually belongs to someone else, such as a landowner

penance The repentance of sins, including confessing, expressing regret for having committed them, and doing something to earn forgiveness

piety A strong belief in and correspondingly fervent practice of religion

pilgrimage A journey undertaken to a specific destination, often for religious purposes

prank A mischievous or humorous trick

pre-Columbian Of or relating to the period before Christopher Columbus arrived in the Americas

procession A group of people moving together in the same direction, especially in a type of celebration

prophecy A prediction about a future event

prophet An individual who acts as the interpreter or conveyer of the will of God and spreads the word to the followers or possible followers of a religion. A prophet can also be a stirring leader or teacher of a religious group. Capitalized it refers to Muhammad.

Protestant A member of a Christian denomination that does not follow the rule of the pope in Rome and is not one of the Eastern Orthodox Churches. Protestant denominations include Anglicans (Episcopalians), Lutherans, Presbyterians, Methodists, Baptists, and many others.

Quran The holy book of Islam

rabbi A Jew who is ordained to lead a Jewish congregation; rabbis are traditionally teachers of Judaism.

reincarnation The belief in some religions that after a person or animal dies, his or her soul will be reborn in another person or animal; it literally means, "to be made flesh again." Many Indian religions such as Hinduism, Sikhism, and Jainism, believe in reincarnation.

repentance To express regret and ask forgiveness for doing something wrong or hurtful.

requiem A Mass for the souls of the dead, especially in the Catholic Church

revel To celebrate in a joyful manner; to take extreme pleasure

ritual A specific action or ceremony typically of religious significance

sacred Connected with God or religious purposes and deemed worthy of veneration and worship

sacrifice Something given up or offered in the name of God, a deity or an ancestor.

shaman A spiritual guide who a community believes has unique powers to tell the future and to heal the sick. Shamans can mediate or cooperate with spirits for a community's advantage. Cultures that practice shamanism are found all over the world still today.

Shia A Muslim sect that believes that Ali, Muhammad's son-in-law, should have succeeded Muhammad as the caliph of Islam; a common sect in Iran but worldwide encompassing only about 15 percent of Muslims

solar calendar A calendar that is based on the time it takes Earth to orbit once around the Sun

solar Related to the Sun

solilunar Relating to both the Sun and Moon

solstice Day of the year when the hours of daylight are longest or shortest. The solstices mark the changing of the seasons–when summer begins in the Northern Hemisphere (about June 22) and winter begins in the Northern Hemisphere (about December 22).

spiritual Of or relating to the human spirit or soul, or to religious belief

Sunni The largest Islamic sect, including about 85 percent of the world's Muslims

supernatural Existing outside the natural world

Talmud The document that encompasses the body of Jewish law and customs

Torah Jewish scriptures, the first five books of the Hebrew scriptures, which serve as the core of Jewish belief

veneration Honoring a god or a saint with specific practices

vigil A period in which a person stays awake to await some event

Vodou A religion rooted in traditional African beliefs that is practiced mostly in Haiti, although it is very popular in the West Indies as well. Outside of Haiti it is called *Vodun*.

Further Resources

■ Books

12 Major World Religions: The Beliefs, Rituals, and Traditions of Humanity's Most Influential Faiths. By Jason Boyett. Published in 2016 by Zephyros Press, Berkeley, Calif. A sound introduction to the world's major religions, including Hinduism, Judaism, and Islam.

Hinduism: A Very Short Introduction, 2nd Ed. By Kim Knott. Published in 2016 by Oxford University Press, Oxford, UK. The revised edition of this compact yet thorough survey of Hinduism provides new information on the impact of technology and social media on Hindus, political developments in India, and other issues.

Judaism (Major World Religions). By Adam Lewinsky. Published in 2017 by Mason Crest, Broomall, Pa. This volume is one in a series exploring the world's major religious traditions. It explores the history, beliefs, and practices of Judaism from ancient times through the present.

Rosh Hashanah. By Julie Murray. Published in 2014 by Buddy Books, Pinehurst, N.C. This compact volume focuses on the holiday of Rosh Hashanah, including its special celebrations.

100 Questions and Answers About Muslim Americans. By the Michigan State University School of Journalism. Published in 2014 by Read the Spirit Books, Canton, Mich. This comprehensive guide to Islamic perspectives on culture, politics, family life, and prayer features a section on holidays.

Maori Warriors. By Ray McClellan. Published in 2012 by Bellwether Media, Minnetonka, Minn. Learn more about Maori culture through the history, strategies, and weapons of the great Maori warriors.

■ Web Sites

BBC. http://www.bbc.co.uk/newsround/15451833. General page of information on Divali that also provides video clips.

The Jewish Virtual Library. http://www.jewishvirtuallibrary.org/rosh-hashanah. Online encyclopedia providing extensive and easy-to-follow explanations of practically every aspect of Judaism. Includes information on important Jewish women, the Holocaust, biographies of famous Jews, and Israel.

National Geographic One-Stop Research. http://www.nationalgeographic.com/onestop. Site by National Geographic allows students to search for information on an endless array of topics on countries around the world. Provides links to photographs, art, games, videos, and lesson plans.

Religious Tolerance.org. http://www.religioustolerance.org. Comprehensive site with information on nearly every world religion, including a wide range of articles and research tools.

Sacred Texts.com. http://www.sacred-texts.com/hin/dutt/index.htm. An abridged version of the sacred text Ramayana that includes the important stories told during the festival of Divali.

ThoughtCo.com. Judaism. https://www.thoughtco.com/what-is-rosh-hashanah-2076484. Site with information about the meaning, liturgy, and customs of Rosh Hashanah.

Virtual Jerusalem. http://www.virtualjerusalem.com/holidays.php. Site with extensive information on all of the Jewish holidays that take place throughout the year.

Te Ara: The Encyclopedia of New Zealand. http://www.teara.govt.nz. Online encyclopedia with information about the country's environment, history, peoples, economy, and geography. More information is being prepared and will be added over time. Entries that relate to the Maori appear in both Maori and English.

Index

Picture Credits